FLUFFING THE CONCRETE

FLUFFING THE CONCRETE

Mack Dryden

Texas Review Press
Huntsville, Texas

SECOND EDITION, 2006

Requests for permission to reproduce material from this work
should be sent to:

Permissions
Texas Review Press
English Department
Sam Houston State University
Huntsville, TX 77341-2146

Cover design by Rick Friesen of Birdbrain Arts

Library of Congress Cataloging-in-Publication Data

Dryden, Mack.
  Fluffing the concrete : making the most of foreign
prison--or anything else / Mack
Dryden. -- 2nd ed.
    p. cm.
  ISBN-13: 978-1-881515-97-5 (pbk. : alk. paper)
  ISBN-10: 1-881515-97-4 (pbk. : alk. paper)
  1. Dryden, Mack. 2. Dryden, Mack--Imprisonment.
3. Comedians--United
States--Biography. I. Title.
  PN2287.D75A3 2006
  792.702'8092--dc22
  [B]
                                    2006028606

FLUFFING THE CONCRETE

To Mom and Dad, who gave me a passion for adventure and a safe place to land

Contents

FLUFFING THE CONCRETE

Chapter One:

Surviving Prison for Dummies

I was led in chains to an African prison cell when I was 24 years old. On a soul-chilling night when many young men my age were cuddling with their wives or girlfriends, I was lying on an icy concrete floor, spooning with a Moroccan thug to avoid freezing to death.

I lay there wide awake and shivering, agonizingly aware that I could spend the rest of my life in a cage for humans not fit for society. Like the massive doors that had clanged shut behind me, an impenetrable steel curtain might well have slammed down after Act One of my life, ending a very short run of freedom and promise. My plans and dreams might live only as the feverish visions of a wasted old American babbling in a lonely corner of a prison yard. The enormity and horror of that thought was too vast for my overloaded brain to process, so I quickly learned to concentrate intensely on the things I could control—when to nibble on the carrot slice I saved from the evening meal, which patch of sunlight to sit in, when to wash my face.

I also learned to take and appreciate whatever good I could find with the bad. My spooning partner's breath could have knocked a camel cross-eyed, but it also warmed a little patch of my scalp. His week-old beard scratched the back of my neck, but his boney thighs took the chill off mine.

Lying there in the dark—literally and figuratively, being totally ignorant of the justice system that ensnared me—I naturally thought of home. I was thankful that my parents still imagined me strolling the beach on the postcard I had sent them from the Spanish coast. If they somehow found out I was in a Moroccan prison, my Mom's huge, tender heart would be gripped by debilitating dread and nearly burst.

My Dad would recover from the gut punch, take a deep breath, clench his fists, stomp around the room railing at third-rate foreign governments and hard-headed, dumb-ass boys, then start trying to arrange a prisoner exchange. He'd take my place in a heartbeat. He'd also think, "Six years of college for *this?*" And who could blame him? A Masters degree doesn't guarantee a split-level with central air, of course; but one would think it might ensure a career path that doesn't include a stretch in a Third World hoosegow.

It's easy to joke about it now, but enduring the long nights I spent at the mercy of a murky foreign justice system was like trying to breathe on the bottom of a tar pit. My world had turned black. There is no Bill of Rights in Morocco, no right of *habeas corpus*. For days I wondered how long I would be behind bars, or if I would even face a judge. Morocco is a hereditary monarchy, so the only thing I knew for sure was that the rights we Americans take for granted didn't apply. I was unsure if I had any rights at all. I didn't even know if I would be allowed to get word to anyone on the outside—I might simply disappear inside a windowless dungeon on a vast continent.

As I prayed for God to drop me a rope ladder,

I made certain promises to Him and to myself. By writing this book and sharing some of the lessons I learned, I'm keeping one of those promises.

*   *   *

Obviously, the experience shaped who I am as a man and taught me things about myself and the world I probably couldn't have learned any other way. I couldn't even talk about the experience for several years after I was safely home. If I talked about it for more than a moment, those horrible feelings of helplessness and fear would roil my guts and I'd have to fight to keep from choking up. I didn't endure a fraction of the horrors many combat veterans have, and yet I now understand why many of them are loathe to talk about their experiences. As tough and courageous as they might be, they know there's a real chance that the horrors will come flooding back and they'll show emotions tough guys aren't supposed to show. They'll also feel real pain—those memories hurt. It's less painful to stay mute.

After a dozen years of new experiences piled up insulation between the present and that awful incident, I was able to talk to close friends and family about it without breaking down. After I began speaking professionally, my wife—recognizing it as a defining moment in my life and full of poignant lessons—urged me to incorporate it into my motivational speeches. Naturally, I resisted. After all, I did go to jail for a crime—not my proudest moment. And most associations and corporations don't seek out jailbirds to inspire the troops. But the more I spoke about goal-achieving, the more I realized that the story lent itself perfectly to the message I try to communicate to my audiences. I realized that more than two decades before I "discovered" the goal-achieving formula successful people have been using for centuries, I instinctively used the same tools and techniques to survive one of my most terrifying challenges.

To achieve that goal, I:

1. Controlled my fears and stresses. A 24-hour job in a foreign prison, believe me. But it's task *Numero Uno* when you embark on achieving a goal. You can't have those incredibly powerful forces dragging you down.

2. Maintained a positive mental attitude. It's a cliché because research has proven it a jillion times: a negative attitude gets negative results, a positive attitude gets positive results. I don't make the rules. It's a law of nature.

3. Identified a very specific target. Surviving and walking out free were my ultimate goals, of course. But I identified a more immediate, specific goal very early, and it definitely saved me from some serious nastiness.

4. Meticulously mapped out a plan. I couldn't afford mistakes, so I went over my plan dozens of times before I . . .

5. Took dramatic action. This was no time to be shy—or threatening. I had to hit the sweet spot right in between. As you'll see, when I decided on my plan of action, I didn't hold back. I pumped the adrenaline and went for the gold.

6. Paid attention to the responses to my actions and listened to anyone who could teach me something. I define an "expert" as anybody who knows something you don't. I listened intently to illiterate 19-year-old thugs who had something to teach me about surviving in that hell-hole. Too often people don't listen to what the world and the *experts* are telling them.

7. Used what I learned to adjust my approach and persevered until I got what I wanted.

I paid attention and acted on what I learned. This is how all goal-achievers ultimately get what they want.

As I said, I take no credit for this ancient guide. I've read books by and about extraordinary goal-achievers from Chopra to Oprah, and they've all followed the same basic steps to reach their objectives. Every successful person from Alexander the Great to Madonna has followed the same fundamental road map to get what he or she wanted. Now, as I attack my various goals, I don't flail away in ten different directions not knowing if I'm getting any closer to my objective. I have a path. It's comforting and motivating to know that I have an iron-clad, time-tested guide to show me the way. If you're tired of flailing, write the guide down and post it where you can see it. That's your first step toward getting what you really want out of life. Or out of a Moroccan jail, as the case may be.

Chapter Two:

Unarmed and Dangerous—Control Is the Key

So how did a mild-mannered 24-year-old native of Moss Point, Mississippi, with an M.A. in Creative Writing and a flair for comedy end up in prison in Africa? Good question. Shocked the hell out of *me*, I can tell you. Ironically, I was led to that unlikely circumstance by two of my Major Collegiate Accomplishments, one of which was surviving being kicked repeatedly by karate champion Chuck Norris.

Yes, *that* Chuck Norris—the actor and one-time U.S. Karate Champion who kicked and punched and tossed bad guys around like Frisbees in his many movies and on TV's "*Walker: Texas Ranger.*" He's the Real Deal, and he wasn't joking when he kicked me. He was mad. He tossed *me* around and humiliated me in front of 200 people. I chose not to fight back. On my list of *People Not to Annoy*, the current Black Belt Karate Champion of the United States of America is perennially in the Top 2. Being humiliated is one thing. Being humiliated *and* knocked unconscious is worse, so I let it go.

Ironically, I came to be kicked in the butt by a karate champion because I was a runt when I was a kid. When I was a senior in high school, I was the size of the average seventh-grader. I took after my Dad. He's only five-foot-five, but there's nothing little about him. *He* always thought he was six-foot four. He passed on his short gene to me, but he gave me so many other things that he actually made me proud of it. If ever there was a living example of the adage that "it's not the size of the dog in the fight but the size of the fight in the dog," it was Herbert Dryden. I knew lots of men well over six feet tall who looked up to my Dad. He's the reason I could never use my small stature as an excuse for anything. He made it sound like a hollow whine.

Being fleet of foot and about half gristle, I was good at sandlot sports in high school; but I was also a 115-pound flea-weight. The guys on our football team wore shoulder pads that outweighed me. So I found a niche. I cut a sapling in the woods and learned to pole vault in my backyard. I went out for the track team and beat the school record with a vault of twelve feet—a dizzying height for a back-water school whose team ran track around garbage cans placed around the football field.

I was eager to excel in something, but assumed that breaking a record no one knew or cared about would be the zenith of my glorious athletic career. Ole Miss, after all, gave scholarships to monstrous jocks who ate snacks roughly the same size as me. Competing in *anything* on the college level seemed an unrealistic notion.

Then, during my freshman year, I stumbled upon an athletic competition in the gym that changed my life. I saw dozens of guys in crisp, white *gis* and colorful belts practicing a startlingly beautiful, exquisitely dangerous art that took my breath away. The action was a blur. A half-dozen matches were being fought in rings marked off only by masking tape on the hardwood gym floor. The competitors would stalk each other for a moment, and then explode into an electrifying flurry of kicks, punches and yells. The spectacle was breathtaking: the speed, the precision, the focus and concentration required of a *karateka* to leap four feet into the air, turn 360 degrees and kick an opponent in the face with a blow so perfectly controlled that it wouldn't crush a grape. I was mesmerized by the power, the control, the intensity of it all.

I was drawn to a match of brown-belts—the rank just below black. One competitor was about six feet tall and 200 pounds. His opponent was a slender little fellow, possibly Indian or Pakistani, about five-feet six inches, who wouldn't tip the scales at more than 140. It seemed like a mismatch, and it was. The bigger guy charged, and the little guy stopped him with a murderous side kick that felled him like a tree. A couple more furious exchanges and the big guy was eliminated. The little guy ate his lunch. I had found my sport.

I joined the Ole Miss Karate Club and fell in love with *tae kwon do*. I felt like a fish that had just discovered water. I had always been a good "little" baseball player, a good "little" sandlot football player, and a horrible "miniature" basketball player. Suddenly I wasn't little anymore. I was just good. Karate fit me like ballet fit Baryshnikov and baseball fit DiMaggio. There was no size requirement. To excel, you simply had to have focus, quickness, agility, dedication, and a willingness to have a cut, scrape, bruise or scab healing up on you somewhere at all times.

I never felt more alive than when I was training, more exhilarated than when I won a competition, or more devastated than when I was defeated. I ate, drank and breathed it for four years. I even dreamt it. One night I dreamt I was sparring against a tough opponent, and the intensity of it jolted me awake. In the dream I had *seen* myself execute a fighting technique that I'd never tried before. I went into the hall of my dormitory at three a.m. and practiced the kick-punch-kick combination for half an hour to see if it felt right and might actually work in competition. It did, and in subsequent tournaments, I scored dozens of points using the technique that literally came to me in a dream.

Karate taught me dozens of life lessons, including how to accept defeat and how to walk away from a fight even if you know you can win it. It also taught me something about control. When you've got it, your destiny is in your own hands. When you lose it, you pay the price.

As a very *green* green belt, I lost it at a tournament in Dallas (ironically, green means you've studied for about a year and aren't a beginner anymore). I had been competing primarily in Mississippi, Louisiana and Tennessee; and we'd been warned that they did things differently in the Great Republic of Texas. I scored around 80 percent of my points with kicks. I could stick a lightning-fast roundhouse kick into an opponent's stomach before he could move his arms to block it. Texans thought kicks were for sissies, and that real men fought with their fists. So well-placed kicks didn't impress Texas judges, which was bad news for those of us who scored primarily with our feet.

The tournament in Dallas was huge by our standards—around 400-500 competitors—so it was quite a coincidence that of the dozen or so referees in as many rings, champion Chuck Norris was assigned to mine. I respected him (what green belt wouldn't?), and thought it was a good sign. Surely a champion of his stature would recognize a well-focused blow whether it was executed by hand or foot.

Shortly after my match started, I nailed my opponent with a kick to the breast-bone and Mr. Norris and two other judges stood there like I had waved a hanky at him. I regrouped, a little frustrated, and decided that maybe they hadn't been in position to see my gorgeously-executed, perfectly-placed roundhouse kick, even though Stevie Wonder would have *sensed* its undeniable beauty and given me a point.

After a couple more nicely executed kicks netted me zilch, I got mad. *Okay, Mr. Norris, you want to see some hands, I'll show you some &*@%$# hands.* I went *ballistic.* I screamed and charged the guy with such fury that he actually blanched. I grabbed a handful of his *gi* and—while pushing to keep him off balance—proceeded to punch him in the ribs, the kidneys, the face, the stomach, the ribs, the stomach, while being vaguely aware of someone yelling "Stop!" I kept hitting him in the ribs, the kidneys, the stomach, *I'll show you some &*@%$# hands,* then someone grabbed onto *my* gi and was yelling 'Stop!' very close to my ear and I felt a foot go *wham-wham-wham* into the seat of my pants and since I could see that my opponent's feet were still attached to him, I got disoriented as Mr. Norris *jerked* me away from the guy and commenced to march me across the ring punctuating every other word with a kick in my flustered little butt: "When I say *stop* (*wham*!), you *stop* (*wham*!), or I'll kick you out of this arena myself *(wham)*! Do you (*wham*!) understand me?!"

My butt went from flustered to chastened. I nodded.

As Alex Trebec would say, that was not the response he was looking for. He gripped my gi and glared at me three inches from my nose.

"I said, 'Do you under*stand* me?!'"

"Yes *sir!*" I yelled, and my words carried very well in that big arena because the two hundred or so people on our end of it had stopped what they were doing to see what was going on. Naturally, I was disheartened and frustrated. I lost the match because I lost the will to fight. I had given the guy my best shots, and I might as well have been trying to shoot a basketball into beer bottle. Nothing worked, so I lost my cool, lost control, and lost the match. I vowed never to do it again. Unfortunately, I broke that vow five years later and paid an even higher price.

Instead of stewing about the defeat and humiliation, I decided to use what I'd learned to improve my hand techniques. I tried to use every setback like that: as an opportunity to get better, to learn something, to get stronger. I had read that successful people don't have 'failures,' only results. They see defeat as an *opportunity*—to learn something, to get tougher, to sharpen their tools. A famous story is told about Thomas Edison, who had been working for years to find the final missing part of the puzzle that would allow one of his most famous inventions to work. One day a young man asked him if all these "failures" discouraged him. Mr. Edison snorted, "Failures? I don't have any failures. Young man, I'll have you know that in only three years I have *discovered* more than 9,000 ways that a light bulb *won't work!*"

The more karate I learned, the more I realized I didn't know. I tried to add to my knowledge and skill a little bit every day, and some of the lessons were painful. I was knocked unconscious. I suffered a bone bruise on my foot that put me on crutches for two weeks. I managed to get a seven-stitch cut in my eyebrow *and* lose a match for first place in about a tenth of a second. I was crushed when my family traveled to watch me compete only to see me lose my first match because I lost concentration.

There were milestones and triumphs, too, of course. During my junior year I earned my brown belt and won first place in every major tournament in the state, becoming the *de facto* brown belt champion of Mississippi.

After my fifth or sixth victory, the president of the state karate association summoned me to his *dojo* in Jackson. Although he didn't tell me the purpose, I suspected that he was going to test me for my black belt and I began training furiously. I drove up on a Saturday, and he told me to get into my gi. We sat facing each other in a darkened room, he asked me a few questions, then told me to stand and to take off my brown belt. He pulled a crisp new black belt from a box and carefully tied it around my waist. I breathed deeply, waited for the bubble in my throat to dissipate, and said, "I trained like a maniac all week. Aren't you going to test me?"

"Test you?" he said. "You've already been tested by every brown belt in the state. They all want you to move up," he grinned, "and start picking on people your own size."

I thought of the five-foot-five-inch man who taught me the difference between size and substance, and I smiled. For the first time, I felt almost as big as my Dad.

Chapter Three:

So Much Blame to Pass Around,

So Little Time

So, earning a black belt in *tae kwon do* karate was one of the Major Collegiate Accomplishments that ultimately led to my being a guest of the Moroccan government. The other was a tad more scholarly.

During my senior year at Ole Miss, just as it seemed I would manage to complete four years of study without a single noteworthy academic achievement, I wrote a short story for my creative writing class that got my professor's attention. He urged me to enter it in the Mississippi Arts Festival, an annual literary competition open to every writer in the state. To you wiseacres: No, a statewide writing contest in Mississippi is not analogous to an Icelandic Surfing Competition. The state that produced William Faulkner, Tennessee Williams, Willie Morris, Barry Hannah, Eudora Welty, John Grisham, and Beth Henley, among many others, still manages for some odd reason to breed more than its share of writers.

Anyway, I won First Place for fiction, owing partially to the fact that none of the above-mentioned writers chose to enter.

Soon after the winners were announced, I got a call from the Second Place winner, Dr. Gordon Weaver, who was heading up the new Center for Writers at the University of Southern Mississippi in Hattiesburg, 200 miles south of Ole Miss. Obviously, the judges found out I was from Moss Point and that Dr. Weaver was a Michigan carpetbagger and voted accordingly. In any case, the very kind and erudite Dr. Weaver congratulated me and asked if I'd be interested in accepting a fellowship to study for a Masters Degree in Creative Writing at USM. Having no desire to enter The Real World at that moment, I gratefully accepted.

My fellowship required that I teach one class of freshman English each semester of my two-year program. Oddly, nobody asked this 22-year-old post-pubescent yahoo if he knew anything about teaching—I didn't. I just got the textbook and waded in on instinct. My first class consisted of 18 freshman "meats," or football players, and two young women who looked as nervous as bunnies in a dog pound. Both coeds transferred within a week. One day the head of the English department invited me into her office to chat about how my teaching was going. I told her I thought I was doing fine, but wondered why I—a wet-behind-the-ears kid with no education credits—was thrown to the meats. She blushed. "We saw that you're also teaching karate," she said. "We thought the athletes might give you, well, a bit more respect."

Ah. Okay. That made sense—kind of. I pictured myself trying to stop a safety blitz by a dozen bull-necked freshmen. Karate *this*, puh-fesser! I'd be helpless. And no staffers ever popped in to check on our safety. We were on our own.

Which is why I ended up in a federal prison in Africa.

Being on our own, we student teachers tended to flock together, and I very naturally fell in with doctoral candidates Paul Ruffin and David Berry. Being single guys from small towns in Mississippi who enjoyed live music, ladies, and language, we bonded and rented a house that we christened "The Deer Camp" so no one would mistake it for a full-time domicile of civilized humans. It brought out our hairier instincts. We used to pee off the back porch while barking just to hear the chain reaction it triggered among the canine population in our neighborhood. We scoured the shower every month just to keep amphibians from colonizing. I once found a pretty little plant with oval leaves growing out of a sponge beside the kitchen sink. A rare female visitor once opened a drawer looking for a fork, saw something move, screamed and evacuated. The premises, I mean.

Today, all three of us are professional, domesticated men who live in spotless homes because we are married to women. But when we lived in The Deer Camp, David and Paul infected me with a bug that I have to this day. Both had traveled in Europe and told tales that made me itch to get on the next plane: searching for a stray student in Rome, camping near the *Louvre* in Paris, riding a water taxi in Venice. I pictured the places they evoked through the golden lens of a Merchant Ivory film. I was hooked. I *ached* to travel to exotic places, eat indigenous food, drink wine with the locals, feel the Mediterranean sun, the English chill, maybe a Swedish nurse.

I earned my M.A., got a job at a shipyard in Pascagoula, and started packing away as much "Europe money" as I could. Paul and David would finish their doctoral work in June, when I would quit my job and the three of us would jump on a plane to invade The Continent—The Three Amigos on a grand adventure.

I quit my job, bought a ticket, signed a handful of traveler's checks and packed a backpack. David handed in the first draft of his dissertation to the review board, who rejected it and insisted on a rewrite. He had to stay in school. Paul, meanwhile, met a beautiful girl, fell in love, and got married, ending his life as we knew it.

Suddenly and unexpectedly, I was bereft of traveling companions. My mother—who had been keeping a stiff upper lip about this loopy plan of mine to wander aimlessly in an alien place—could hardly contain her joy. My Dad—who had wanted to go on such an adventure since he was a teenager—asked me what I was going to do. My Mom glared a hole in Dad for even suggesting that there might be an alternative to abandoning this rash, solo leap off the edge of the planet.

I had been planning and working for this too long to abort the mission. And I knew if I didn't go when I had a ticket, a thousand dollars and nothing to stop me, I'd probably never go. Life would intervene. I'd get a job, find a soul-mate, buy a house, get a weed-wacker and a six-pack and settle for watching the Wide World from my La-Z-Boy.

I told them I was going by myself. They didn't stop me, so my parents join Paul and David on the list of people responsible for me languishing in a Moroccan jail.

Chapter Four:

Go Where the Dirhams Are

Looking out the window of the Icelandic Air plane at rolling farmland and ancient stone fences, I realized I'd achieved my first post-college goal: I had actually made it to Europe with a backpack and a bankroll. I had tucked any fears I had behind my attitude that thousands of Americans had gone to Europe in the 1940's and survived it even though people were *shooting* at them—a problem I didn't think I'd have.

Now my goal was to make the most of it—to see and smell and feel and hear and experience as much as I possibly could while I was there. I didn't know how long that would be because I didn't know how long a thousand 1973 dollars would last. As it turned out, $200 of it didn't even last until I landed in Luxembourg. There was an oil embargo, and the dollar lost about 20% of its value before I could cash a single traveler's check (my friends won't be surprised by this—I once lost money in Southern California real estate).

I had bought a Eurail Pass before I left the U.S., so for two months I rode the Magic Carpet: present it, hop on any train on the Continent, and just *go*. I camped in Luxembourg for a few days with a guy from Chicago who'd bought a box of motorcycle and was assembling it from scratch. I slept in a park in Amsterdam with hundreds of other backpackers. I rocked at a pop festival in Frankfurt, circled the Coliseum in Rome and rode the water-buses of Venice. I spread out my sleeping bag in a bean field near Pisa, jumped a ferry from Italy's toe to Sicily, and dove for sea urchins off the islands of Sardinia and Corsica. I slept on a beach in Spain, ran with the bulls in Pamplona, and partied with a one-eyed Dutchman in Lisbon. (Okay, I didn't *exactly* run with the bulls in Pamplona. I climbed a tree and dangled *over* the bulls in Pamplona—but I did get punched out by a Spaniard who hadn't had quite as much wine as I had, so I *looked* like I'd been run over by a bull. The Festival of San Fermin has rules: if somebody with a goatskin full of wine yells for you to line up with some other grape-colored revelers and open your mouth, you have to—it's a local ordinance).

It must seem inconceivable today that anyone could travel as much as I did on my meager bankroll and even have money left over after two months, but I managed it. There were *thousands* of young American backpackers criss-crossing Europe that summer, and we tended to find each other, share resources and generally help each other out. I got lots of free meals, drinks, rides, and accommodations, and even earned a few dollars doing little chores like guarding a motorcycle or feeding a dog or carrying a bathtub up a flight of stairs. I made friends with the locals, too, so there were quite a few days that I didn't spend a *peseta*.

After two months on the road, I had learned quite a bit about surviving as a backpacker in Europe—and had some insight as to how to work the system. I saw a man digging a trench to lay some pipe in his yard outside Heidelberg. Using charades and my baby German I offered to help him dig it, and I earned the equivalent of about $30 that day. I got $20 for picking up a mound of bottles behind a Belgian bar, I made a few bucks chopping weeds at a campground. And so it went until I got to Amsterdam in mid August, just when hundreds of broke and sunburned American students were gathering to fly back to school in the States—weighed down with tons of souvenirs, gear, and even road-worthy vehicles.

I went to the biggest campground in the city and found it packed with young Americans eager to get *anything* for stuff they'd have to throw away anyway. I bought everything from backpacks and hiking boots to camp stoves and a 1964 Volkswagen van with Dutch plates—all for pennies on the dollar. I packed my new van and puttered off to make a pleasant little loop through Rotterdam, Cologne and Antwerp, where I sold everything I didn't want, easily paying for the van and having gas money left over. I was working the system, but privation and a growling gut loomed just over the next rise in the *Autobahn.* With the blustery north wind biting deeper every day, I had to come up with a longer-term plan to keep *bratwurst* in my belly and gas in the tank.

I had heard that *le vendange*—the French grape harvest—was beginning in September, and that a healthy fellow could make some pretty good money, so I headed south. I tried a couple of places that had already hired their crews, and was beginning to think I was too late. I parked my van in the tiny village of Blaye near Bordeaux to have a bite to eat when a slightly desperate man in muddy boots walked over and asked me if I wanted to make some quick money. Some pickers had abruptly left him, and he had to get his grapes in quickly or the harvest would be ruined. He was hiring anybody with a heartbeat, and I qualified. It was the hardest physical labor I've ever done, and I've done some pretty hard labor. Try duck-walking for eight hours in mud and you'll get the idea. It was brutal, but the food was terrific and the pay not bad.

I picked grapes for three weeks to get a little stash together, but my aching bones—and itchy feet—said there had to be a better way.

Picking grapes near Bordeaux. It's not quite as romantic as it seems. Try duck-walking in mud for eight hours and you'll get the idea.

A couple of weeks later at a campground near Lyon, I picked up a German couple who were headed back to Munich after a month-long journey through Spain and Morocco. They both wore necklaces of so-called "African trade beads" that were hip among the young travelers of the day. The cylindrical glass beads of intricate design—properly called *millefiori,* Italian for *a thousand flowers*—were made primarily in Venice from the late 1700's to the 20ᵗʰ century, and were used as money in Africa to buy everything from gold to slaves. During the psychedelic Sixties and Seventies, young travelers wore them as a badge declaring they had completed the *de riguer* journey to Morocco to experience the Third World country most accessible to West Europeans—and to legally smoke hashish in the fabled region known as *Ketama.* Hash was easily procured in the rest of the country as well, along with a plethora of *legal* exotic goods like leather, beads and fabrics that decorated the colorful *medinas*, or Old Towns, of storied cities like Casablanca, Fez, and Marrakech; so in the mind-expanding "back to the earth" Seventies, Morocco was a prime destination for long-haired youths in tie-dyed shirts and sandals, meaning pretty much everybody under thirty.

Still in my merchant mode, I asked the couple if they'd like to sell their beads. They laughed and said no, but that they wished they'd bought more because they could have sold them all.

Actually, he said, "Vee coot haff solt effry vun of zem," but who am I to make fun? I know only about ten phrases in German, including "One beer, please," and "Quick—where's the mens' room?" But, however he said it, the meaning was clear: *Go South, Young Man, and Buy Beads.* Add these hitchhikers to the list of people responsible for me going to the slammer in a Third World country.

Chapter Five:

Feeling Even Stranger in a Strange Land

Two weeks later I wheeled my van into Algeciras, Spain, in the shadow of the great Rock of Gibraltar, which is British, which just rankles the hell out of the Spaniards, who absolutely despise the idea that a foreign government can claim a tiny hunk of land on their very own coastline. Of course, they think it's just *splendido* that they claim the towns of Melilla and Ceuta, tiny hunks of land on the coast of Morocco, just across the Strait. That's different, because *everybody* colonized Africa when it was trendy. Remember the *Belgian* Congo? I've been to Belgium. It's the size of the average American shopping mall. Heck, Delaware probably had a territory over there sometime or other—what's your *problemo?*

Anyway, the cheapest way to Morocco is to take the ferry from Spain to, well, Spain. I didn't want to take my van on my first excursion to such an alien place, so I paid a guy a few *pesetas* to park it behind his mechanic shop, put a few necessities in my backpack and got on a ferry.

The hideous little port burg of Ceuta is completely surrounded by water and Morocco, so calling it a "border town" is like calling Bermuda "ocean adjacent." It's nothing *but* border. Getting through the actual border—back then, anyway—was a piece of *flan*. The Spanish were happy to get rid of *peseta*-pinchers like me, and the Moroccans were thrilled to get anybody who wore jeans worth more than most of them made in a month.

Past the border, I caught a rattletrap bus to the first Moroccan city bigger than a horse trough, Tétouan, whose motto is "At Least We're Not Ceuta." Its proximity to Ceuta gives it the same border-

Constrastingly, in America we use trucks to carry our livestock. Who needed hashish when such visions as this abounded?

town charm, as much of the local economy is built around smuggling and ripping off visitors. In Tétouan—which, to be fair, has its charm—I began my education in how to safely navigate the mean, poor, fascinating streets of a Third World country. Being, coincidentally, the only blue-eyed white guy in Tétouan that night, I attracted lots of attention and had to be on constant alert. Kids swarmed me asking for handouts, and young men waded through them shooing them off and giving me their sales pitches: "Hey, you German? Dutch? American? You want place to stay? I got best deal in Tétouan.

You want good food, I know best place, very clean, cheap, cheap. You want hashish? Come on, good price, I get you good price."

I didn't feel in constant physical danger, because I knew the Moroccan king and his honchos made fertilizer out of violent criminals—particularly those who would tarnish the country's reputation as a safe place for Westerners to unload their cash. On the other hand, I knew there was no shortage of people who would happily separate me from all my money and worldly possessions and maybe even a body part if I put on blinders and got sloppy.

Since I already felt somewhere between "jumpy" and "paranoid," smoking hashish would definitely fall into the category of "sloppy." I can't even drink a beer in the afternoon without keeling over for a nap. I could barely deal with this bizarre situation *sober*. If I got fuzzy-brained on some powerful Atlas Mountain gonzo goo, I might wake up naked in the desert trying to remember the license plate of the camel that trampled me. Or my addled brain might be so flooded with undying affection for my wonderful new friends that I might just *give* them everything. I was already seeing things that *resembled* hallucinations—when's the last time *you* saw two burly guys in military uniforms and manly mustaches walk across the street together holding hands like Jack and Jill? Spotting a hookah-puffing caterpillar wouldn't have surprised me at that point.

Besides, word travels fast in small-town Mississippi, and I'd rather have died than embarrass my parents with a drug rap. I just couldn't take the chance, particularly in a lovely resort destination like Tétouan. So I picked the guy who seemed to know the most English ("You like Jimi Hendrix?"), and for about fifty cents hired him to take me to the safest places to sleep and eat. He was mystified when I passed on the hashish, since that's what most "Europeans" came down there for. After trying for a good fifteen minutes to make him understand what *allergic* meant—French being the second language for both of us—I just said I didn't like it.

My accommodations in Tétouan were memorable because I wasn't given a key to my room. The innkeeper simply pulled the doorknob off my door and handed it to me, explaining that if I wanted a room with a fancy-schmancy *key* I'd have to pay a lot more.

I don't mean to poke fun at the Moroccans and their lower standard of living. I'm grateful that my experience in their country shaped who I am in many ways. I don't take for granted the incredible luxuries that we Americans enjoy, and I abhor the sinful waste I see every day in our country. I learned that the absence of electricity, running water, and telephones doesn't equal misery or even poverty, and that human kindness can flourish in the most unlikely places. I learned that because people do things differently in other places doesn't make them wrong, and I saw things I could never spin from my imagination.

I saw live goats, sheep and chickens tied to the tops of buses along with the luggage, and I once saw a camel and a comically-overmatched calf pulling *the same* plow over a field that seemed to be covered with litter. I learned later that farmers plow in paper and other trash for the meager nutrients.

I saw scribes sitting on blankets displaying their crisp writing papers and shiny pens. Families would walk for miles from the hills to have a letter read by a scribe, who would laugh and growl and gesticulate to make it memorable—and to make sure they came back to him with the next letter. They'd then watch mesmerized as with wonderfully mysterious sweeps of his pen he turned their very words into an intimate chat with a loved one hundreds or even thousands of miles away. To them it was magic.

I saw a man draw a crowd for the reading of an exciting chapter from a book, swinging an imaginary sword and riding an invisible horse. Later, children sat wide-eyed and grown men gasped and shuddered as he read.

I once got a close-up look at the muzzle of an AK-47 after I argued briefly with a border guard. I also had a dagger pressed to my throat when a shopkeeper thought I had talked another American out of buying a purse from him.

Sleeping in my van in the country-side, I'd often awake from one dream only to feel I had drifted into another.

I slept in my van in a field one night and awoke to see the upside-down face of a camel chewing its cud three feet from my face.

I watched a man auction off every part of a bleating goat tied to a post before he slaughtered it and distributed the pieces. Nobody asked if it was fresh.

I watched a dentist extract a man's tooth in his "office"—a blanket on which his spotless instruments were proudly displayed.

In a bath-house in Marrakech warmed by perpetual wood fires in the basement, I was hand-washed head to toe by a big guy with a mustache who did a very workmanlike job, scrubbing my most sensitive area only slightly more gingerly than he might wash a zucchini.

I saw pedestrians walking past a dead man on a busy, dusty street in Meknès. I passed the same way an hour later and the body hadn't stirred.

At a street carnival, I saw a human-powered, wooden Ferris wheel about ten feet high that could carry four people on its two seats. The riders screamed as if they were going sixty upside-down on a roller coaster at Six Flags.

In the mountains I once stopped near the camp of a young government geologist who invited me to dinner. He said four or five words to his teenage assistant, who trotted over a hill without a word and trotted back two hours later with a sack of cookies.

Merchants specialized: at one shop about a dozen cow heads stared at passersby from unrefrigerated shelves, their huge, slug-like tongues displayed beside them. Another sold nothing but well-scrubbed one-quart motor oil cans with the top cut out and a wire handle on top so it could be used as a bucket. Every city had at least one man who made sandals and water vessels from discarded tires, one who walked through the *souq*, or marketplace, sharpening knives and scissors, and one who carried a goat-skin tank on his back, selling drinks of water from gleaming brass ladles.

One night on a passenger train from Casablanca to Rabat, a man pulled my backpack from under my sleeping head and jumped off the train as it pulled from a station, knowing I couldn't chase him into unknown territory in the dark. Most of my valuables, fortunately, were in a pouch under my shirt. I tried to be philosophical: the guy probably had a couple of hungry kids, and my Swiss army pack probably doubled his income that quarter.

Though I wore faded jeans and flannel shirt and was barely making a living, to most Moroccans I was a "rich Westerner"—as conspicuous as an ostrich in a coffee shop—so naturally I attracted the criminal element. But for every unsavory encounter I had with a Moroccan, I had another that demonstrated the true warmth and generosity of the Moroccan people. One memorable incident occurred on my second trip to Morocco. I had done quite well buying beads in the *souqs*, taking them back to Europe and selling them in campgrounds and on the streets near tourist attractions like the *Louvre*. I routinely got $20 for beads that cost me about a quarter, so the markup was pretty good.

Boys are boys everywhere. This ragtag gaggle near Rabat reminded me of the bunch I ran with back in Mississippi—funny, friendly, and curious. Note the sadly deflated soccer ball they were trying to play with

But I digress—back to the warmth and generosity of the Moroccan people.

On my second trip to Morocco, I took the van, thinking that I could save a few bucks on lodging and transport more merchandise. Bedding down beside a pretty little creek in the mountains instead of in a flea-infested room in a city also had its appeal. I enjoyed camping in my van in the hinterlands, but the price of gasoline ultimately made it impractical. Still, I'm glad I motored through Morocco. Otherwise I wouldn't have a particularly amazing story illustrating the aforementioned warmth and generosity I encountered.

I blew a tire in Meknès and found a repair shop. I bought a new tube and told the mechanic I was going to look around the *souq* while he installed it. When I came back, the tire was fixed and there were a couple of hours of daylight, so I decided to move on. The next day, when Meknès was 60 miles behind me, the tire blew out again and I limped into a mountain village that fortunately had a garage.

I told the friendly young owner who spoke simple French like me that I couldn't understand it because I'd had it fixed the day before in Meknès. "Did you watch him repair it?" he asked. I told him no, I'd gone to do some errands. The pitying look he gave me said, "How did you Americans conquer the world being such naïve knuckleheads?" He took off my tire and found what he expected—an ancient tube with an absolutely cartoonish mosaic of at least 20 patches on it. We were both amazed that it had held up for 60 miles.

I stomped, I kicked, I wished a lifetime of diarrhea and itchy rashes on the mechanic who duped me. Even as I was venting to the mountains, the young mechanic tried to calm me down, telling me not to worry, that he'd make everything okay. He told me he was embarrassed by his dishonest countryman and that he wanted to make up for my loss. When he was done, I was the one who was embarrassed.

He replaced the tube with a new one. He replaced my worn wiper blades. He replaced a turn-signal bulb and tweaked my engine—and he adamantly refused any payment. He would take nothing. Not a *dirham*. Then—just to pile on the guilt—he insisted that I come to his home and have dinner with him and his family. He closed the garage and we walked a hundred yards or so through a collection of neat little mud homes, and friendly people in traditional dress greeted us both along the way. Two young girls smiled shyly at me as they pulled buckets up from a well—the village water supply.

His little two-room home was devoid of furniture and had no running water or electricity. But it was spotless, and colorful blankets folded neatly along the walls and delectable cooking aromas made it quite cozy and inviting. His smiling, chubby little wife—who had a curly-haired, giggling baby girl on her hip—greeted me warmly, even though her husband hadn't warned her that he was dragging home a scruffy foreigner for dinner. Her bright, sincere smile made it clear that I had honored them with my presence, As soon as the baby saw her father, she squirmed from her mother's arms and toddled over to be picked up and nuzzled by her proud pop.

Presently we had a large bowl of delicious vegetables, lamb and *cous-cous* on the floor between us. We sat on blankets and—using the traditional piece of pita-like bread as a "grabber"—picked the food out of the communal bowl. Throughout the meal, their daughter reminded me that we really are a Brotherhood of Man: she climbed over us and giggled and grabbed everything in sight—exactly like two-year-olds were doing that very moment in Tokyo and Brussels and Amarillo. Their obvious love for each other and their kindnesses toward me reaffirmed my belief in the basic good will of humans everywhere.

As we were saying our goodbyes, I gave my host a pocketknife that I had bought in Germany, with an apology for the meagerness of my gift in light of his overwhelming hospitality. You'd have thought I gave him a Mercedes. I thought I was going to have to stab him with it to make him take it. He practically sobbed at my generosity (I didn't have the heart to tell him I always carried one for my own use and usually kept three or four for barter). After warm farewells and wishes of good fortune, I drove into the mountains on my new tire and with my new attitude. As I lay under the stars that night reflecting on the day's events, I even rescinded the hex I had thrown on the Meknès mechanic.

Chapter Six:

Screwing Up in Three Languages

Being fairly simple when it comes to business, I had a fairly simple business plan:

1) Buy stuff cheap
2) Make it look more expensive
3) Sell it for a lot more than you pay for it
4) Trade only in cash
5) Don't tell any nosey governments about it
6) Keep moving.

One would think that buying stuff cheap in economically-depressed, Third-World Morocco would be simple, but there was a lot to learn. Nothing had a price tag on it, of course, so arriving at the final sales price was a totally improvisational exercise. A typical scenario: Engilbert, a German backpacker, stops at a leather shop and looks at a nice pair of sandals. After determining the tourist's nationality, the merchant, Lahbib, tells Engilbert that he's a very lucky guy, because he likes Germans better than any of the Europeans, and will give him a 10% discount just for being from the Fatherland. Besides that, he says, Germans obviously have very keen eyes for quality, because the sandals that caught

Engilbert's attention were made by the finest leather craftsman in Marrakech, whose work is so highly prized that Lahbib can only afford to buy one or two pair a year for his shop. But because Lahbib has a special place in his heart for Germans, he's going to sacrifice this outstanding pair of handcrafted beauties to Engilbert for the low-low special Hands-Across-the Vater-Deutschland-Is-Great discount price of only 100 *dirham,* or about $25. Then he leans in conspiratorially and tells Engilbert that he sold an identical pair last month to an arrogant Frenchman for forty bucks, snerk-snerk.

Engilbert, being no dummy, offers Lahbib $15. The merchant looks heartbroken and hurt, explaining that he has a wife, three kids and a donkey to feed, and that he couldn't possibly let go of the sandals for less than $23, or his ass might starve. The German shrugs and says he could go as high as $20. After a dramatic sigh, Lahbib accepts the $20 with a shake of his head, and Engilbert walks away happy, thinking he's gotten the best of this poor, simple merchant, who of course just yesterday bought ten pairs of those exact same sandals from his buddy Waffi for 50 cents a pair, and sold a pair to Fadma the rug merchant for a buck and a half just this morning.

When I first started buying, I assumed that the merchants would start the negotiations at about twice the fair price. I wasted a lot of unnecessary *dirham* before I realized that they usually started off closer to ten times the amount they'd settle for. Which makes perfect sense: why not swing for the fence if you've got nothing to lose? If a spoiled American traveling on Daddy's money will pay a dollar for a five-cent trinket, he might pay ten. So after awhile I learned how to disarm a merchant from the beginning by getting a laugh, and letting him know I hadn't just stumbled off the ferry. "How much for this shirt?" I'd ask in French. The merchant would size me up quickly, assume I had much more money than street smarts, and say, "One hundred dirham." I would chuckle and say, "No, no, my friend, you misunderstand. I meant the price for one shirt, not twenty." This usually elicited a chuckle, and we could then get down to business.

On one of my trips, I made a dumb mistake that still gives me chills. I met a young American couple from Michigan in the *souq* in Rabat, and they were of course fascinated that I had spent so much time in the country. We sat and had tea in a café, and they grilled me about my gypsy lifestyle and where I sold my goods and so on. I don't remember the particulars of our conversation, but I suspect that I poured on the Intrepid World Traveler bit pretty thick. A little later, we were exploring the *souq* when the girl found me and asked me to look at something in a shop. I went in and looked at a wool cape she was interested in buying. "He wants forty *dirham* for it," she said, "but I don't know if that's a good price. You're an expert, what do you think?"

Naturally, as a 23-year-old *expert*, I squared my jaw like a tough and seasoned adventurer who's accustomed to trading with the natives in exotic and hostile environments, and very coolly said to the shopkeeper, "How about thirty dirham?" He walked straight at me with a murderous look in his eye and pinned me against a wall, arranging his body so no one else could see the dagger he pressed under my chin. In a hoarse whisper, he snarled, "If you ever interfere in my business again, you pig, I will cut your throat."

I thought the situation called for sincerity, so I said exactly what I was truly thinking: "I believe you." I had never actually had a blade pressed to my neck in anger, so I was also feeling like wetting myself. I didn't want to share that part, so I told him I was very sorry. He wasn't in a forgiving mood, since the potential buyers had bolted at the first sign of trouble; but, thankfully, he lowered the blade and pushed me out of his shop, unscathed but chastened.

Talk about pride before a fall. I had been full of swagger, and I arrogantly blew a sale for a guy who was struggling to get by. I was lucky that he didn't cut my gizzard out on the spot. I've often regretted my *faux pas*, but never forgotten or repeated it. Hard-learned lessons are by far the most memorable, I've found.

*   *   *

On my first buying trip, I vastly underestimated the amount of inventory I'd need and made some impractical choices. The shirts, purses, sandals and belts were just too bulky to pack and hard to carry for an itinerant merchant like me. I vowed that when I returned I'd go in search of the single item that gave me the idea in the first place—trade beads.

Back in Spain, I headed northeast up the Mediterranean coast and parked my van in campsites in Malaga, Benidorm, and Valencia, seeing the sights and selling a few things every day to keep me in food, gas, and beer money. If you're a business-minded person, you're probably wondering why I didn't run my business more like a *business* so I could make more money. The simple answer is that I wasn't in Europe to run a business. I was there to travel, to see the world, to experience exotic cultures, have adventures, meet interesting people, be awestruck by amazing works of art and architectural wonders most people would only see in history books or travel magazines. And I didn't really need that much money, because all I wanted to collect was memories. I couldn't be burdened with knick-knacks and spiffy clothes. My blue jeans and khaki or plaid shirts served me very well just

about everywhere I wanted to go. The only ε
I can think of is when I was still backpac
tried to hitch-hike across France. Bad idea. ᵢᵥ
told me that to the French, inviting a stranger into
your vehicle was the same as inviting one into your
house. It just wasn't done.

I probably would have had the same experience had I been wearing a tuxedo; but, whatever
the reason, the only drivers who would pick me up
were gay men. Talk about your colorful memories.
Once I told a truck driver who'd picked me up that
I was headed for Avignon, and he told me I should
go to Paris instead and have some fun. I told him I
wanted to earn a little more money before I went to
Paris. He laughed and said I didn't need any money,
that I already had all I needed to get by in Paris.
Then he reached over and poked me in *The Only
Thing I Needed* to get by in Paris. I squirmed out of
reach, and he let me off at the next village, which
consisted of about four houses, a post office, and a
tiny grocery that would open only if you fetched an
old lady from one of the houses.

I spread my sleeping bag in a bean field that
night. I got up the next day and stuck my thumb
out around 7 a.m., when the first of approximately
300 uppity heterosexual French drivers passed me
without even waving. I stood by the road all day.
Just before dusk, I walked into town and bought
something to eat from the old lady, then trudged
back to the bean field and went to sleep. The next
morning, another gay guy picked me up, and I kept
my pack on my lap for about fifty miles.

Around dusk that night, The Man of Few Words
pulled over. I got in, he said, "*Ou allez-vous?*" (*where
are you going?*), I said, "Avignon," he scratched off
and we went hurtling through the dark on a wind-
ing road at frightening velocity. I was just thrilled
to be in a vehicle and moving forward, so I gritted
my teeth, held on, and kept my mouth shut. After

about twenty miles of driving like Satan's getaway driver in complete silence, he abruptly pulled off the highway onto a dirt road, and I thought, "Uh oh. This just can't be good." Discreetly, I opened my pocketknife and held it beside my leg.

He parked in some heavy brush, cut the engine, pulled out a pack of smokes and said, "Cigarette?"

"*Merci, non,*" *(no, thanks)* I said, shifting into a defensive position and watching his every twitch.

He flicked on a lighter, and his hand shook so violently the flame had a hard time connecting with the target.

"Homosexual?" *(you gay?)* he said.

I hesitated, because I didn't know if disappointing news was going to trigger rude behavior in this guy. But both his hands were in sight, I didn't see a weapon, and I was confident I could bury three-inches of tempered steel in him somewhere before he did much damage to me. So I said, "*Je regrette, mon ami, mais no,*" *(sorry, my friend, but no)* and tensed for action.

"*Tant pis,*" *(the hell with it)* he said, and started the car. *Fan-frickin'-tastic,* I thought. He slammed it into reverse, then raced forward, kicking up dirt as he powered through the brush. We squealed onto the asphalt and blasted into the blackness again, my life and limbs in the hands of a frustrated race-car driver who was now sexually frustrated as well. At the next crossroad, he made a rubber-burning U-turn, screeched to a stop, and shrugged as if to say, "Whattya want, bus service?" I got out without a word. I wasn't about to thank him for abandoning me in the middle of nowhere after dark. When his taillights disappeared, I found myself in darkness as inky as I had ever experienced. I was in the middle of the country, the only visible light seeping from stars in a moonless sky. I squinted into the darkness, and started looking for a place to spread my bag. Not a single car passed, and I literally couldn't see more than a foot or two in front of me. Literally feeling my way, I baby-stepped away from the road, praying I wouldn't flail into barbed wire, stumble into a sleeping bull, or fall into a quarry. I eventually found a flat, dry spot with a little spring to it, spread my bag and slept. I awoke the next morning in a hay field, walked to the road and stuck my thumb out, trolling for homosexuals.

I admit that attempting to hitchhike across France wasn't the most intelligent move I ever made, but at least it resulted in colorful memories. But I digress. Before I took you hurtling through the French countryside with various gay men *(so many tangents, so little time)*, we were on the eastern Mediterranean coast of Spain—the Costa Blanca. I was in that sun-drenched part of the world when I learned another painful lesson. Having never been shamed by generosity before, I had no idea how scalding the sting could be.

In Valencia, I saw advertisements for trips to the Spanish-owned Balearic Islands—Majorca, Ibiza, and three smaller ones—which were two or three hours away by ferry and definitely off the beaten path for most young travelers, so of course I had to see them. I found a safe place to leave the van, grabbed my trusty pack and sleeping bag, and got a ferry ticket to Ibiza. I took an early boat and was on the island by noon.

I took a bus tour and got an overview of the rocky, ancient land that had been settled by all the major powers from the Romans to the Moors, attacked by pirates and finally transformed into a lovely beach getaway. I walked the quaint streets of the main town, Eivissa, and started looking for a place to stay. I priced the rooms at a couple of hotels and was shocked at how expensive they were. So I started looking for a place to spread my bag for the night. I could grab some fruit and cheese in a shop, and there were restrooms and public showers on the beach, so the necessities were available.

I tried to walk up the backstreets, but realized that the town was surrounded by a fenced military installation, so I couldn't walk far without hitting the fence. Most towns have a dense downtown, surrounded by areas with vacant lots and buildings, buildings under construction, railroad yards, etc., but this place had no "outlying area." There were city streets and a ten-foot hurricane fence, and no good place to throw a bag for the night without drawing unwanted attention from the police. There was no alternative, so I bit the bullet and checked into the most reasonably-priced place I could find, a charming little hotel a block from the beach.

I dropped my stuff in the room and went out for a sunset stroll on the beach and to look for a cheap and cheerful place to eat. I had walked a few hundred yards when I saw a big beach pavilion of some kind and went to explore it. When I got there, I realized it was unoccupied because it was under construction, and there were approximately 400 nooks, crannies, and dry spots that were calling out to me and my sleeping bag, "Unroll here! Make yourself at home! You're the only occupant! We'll watch your stuff!" Not only that, but waves were lapping against the pilings, so I would be gently transported into Dreamland by the ocean's lullaby. For free. I had to get out of that hotel.

On the walk back, I realized that the only way out would be a white lie. "I changed my mind" wouldn't be a refundable excuse, I didn't think. The lie would be harmless, I told myself, because I hadn't mussed the bed, used the toilet, or even sat in a chair, so I really wouldn't be costing the hotel anything or causing them any inconvenience. So I walked to the front desk and told the young desk clerk my tale of woe: I had set my little satchel on the seawall for just a few seconds to take a photo for some tourists, and when I got back my wallet had been stolen. I had my passport, but no money to get back to the mainland where I had left traveler's checks for safe-keeping. So if I could just get my money back, I could buy a ticket back to Valencia the next morning.

The young man looked very concerned and told me to wait a moment, he would have to confer with the owner, Señor Ramirez. My Spanish wasn't very good, but I thought he also said he didn't think Señor Ramirez would agree to what I proposed. I was practicing my indignant expression when a short, kindly-looking gentleman about eighty years old came to the desk looking like he had just heard very distressing news. With a combination of the little English he knew and the little Spanish I knew, he confirmed what his desk clerk had told him: my money had been stolen on the beach, in his town, on his island, where I was a guest. He was horrified, and of course I was immediately shamed for having lied. I told him it was all right, if I could just get my money back, I could sleep on the beach and get on the ferry in—

"*Non!*" he said, very emphatically. "Impossible." He said he was shocked and embarrassed that someone had stolen from me, and apologized on behalf of the entire island. He said he would not only give me my money back, but he insisted that I stay in the room for free, as his guest. By then, of course, I was feeling rotten for lying to this wonderful little man. But he was just *starting* to make me feel rotten. He spoke to his desk clerk, who went to the register and got the money I had given him for the room (probably $50 or so, which represented nearly a week's worth of usual expenses for me), plus $20 to help me get back to the mainland. "Oh, no!" I protested, feeling as low as worm puke. This was quickly snowballing out of control. I tried to give the extra $20 back to the employee, but Señor

Ramirez stepped in, grabbed the money, closed my hand over it and shook his finger in my face. "You kip or I am being mad to you," he said. I didn't want him being mad to me, so I kipped it.

Then he spoke to his employee and disappeared into the back. The employee told me that dinner would be served at 7 p.m. and Señor Ramirez insisted that I be there.

I made myself as presentable as possible and went to dinner at the appointed time. A waiter greeted me warmly and told me that I was Señor Ramirez's special guest for dinner. He said it was his job to make sure I had everything I needed, so I shouldn't hesitate to ask for anything at all. I was beginning to choke on my own lie and didn't think I could force down a grape. The waiter brought me a salad and a seafood appetizer, then asked me to make my wine selection from the bottles on a cart he rolled over to my table. I said I couldn't possibly accept wine, too. The waiter looked over his shoulder, then leaned down and whispered, "Señor Ramirez will be very upset if you refuse his hospitality."

To make a painful story short, I have never dined so sumptuously and enjoyed it less. The food was exquisite, the wine perfect, yet every bite and sip went down with a bitter twinge of remorse. During dessert, Señor Ramirez came to my table and asked if the meal had been satisfactory. I did my best to express how deeply his generosity had moved me, but he waved off my thanks and said he hoped that I would not have bad memories of his beloved island. I assured him I would treasure the memory of my stay, and he wished me luck and said good night.

I obviously do treasure the memory and hope by telling the story to be redeemed for my sin in some way. Perhaps someone will read of Señor Ramirez and be inspired to choose truth over falsehood, or to extend a helping hand to someone in true need.

Back on the mainland, I headed farther north and found a campground outside of Barcelona, where I set up business and headquartered to explore the city. When I handed the campground manager my passport, he smiled and said, "Ah, American! Watergate bad, eh?" Um, yeah, I said, Watergate is very bad. The scandal was international news, of course, and I had been following it when I could find a copy of the English-language *International Tribune.* It was the first thing many people would bring up when they found out I was an American, and I understood why: the most powerful people in the most powerful nation on earth were being brought down, and average folks love to see the mighty fall, whether they're people or nations. I couldn't help but be embarrassed by it, but there wasn't much I could do. "Nixon go to jail, eh?" he said with his big grin. Every time he saw me, he'd make some Watergate-related comment. A couple of times he showed me Spanish newspaper articles with photos of Nixon and Agnew and various other players in the debacle, and he always had a grin and a comment: "They think they don't get catched, eh?"

I wanted to say, "Yeah, but at least we can kick our president out if he misbehaves. Why don't you throw out *El Caudillo?" (The Leader)* referring to Francisco Franco, who was then enjoying his 37th year as the authoritarian leader. But in 1973 Spain, if you were prudent you didn't make disparaging comments about the government. Franco constantly reminded the populace who was in power by deploying his *Guardia Civil* in pairs on practically every other street corner. At the train stations, you might see two or three pairs of these scary-looking guys in their dark green uniforms, jodhpurs, stormtrooper boots and flat-backed, black patent-leather hats—and they all carried submachine guns. The sight would give anybody who'd grown up in a democracy a cold chill. Sure, American police wear sidearms. But can you imagine five or six pairs of cops carrying *submachine guns* patrolling Times Square or the Washington Mall?

I was in a small town in Spain when Franco's nominal successor, Luis Carrero Blanco, was assassinated in Madrid, and the streets emptied for two days. People stayed indoors and the town just shut down amid the tense uncertainty of what might follow. The assassins took no chances that this fellow might survive. They exploded a bomb under his car, which landed on top of a five-story building. They found just enough of his body to positively identify him, and his bodyguard's body wasn't found at all. This was clearly not intended as a warning shot. Someone had obviously had it up to *here* with Franco-style rule.

Since the Spanish had enough problems, I saw no reason to remind this affable campground manager that I lived in a democracy and could say anything about Nixon I wanted to. If he said something nasty about Franco, he could disappear, which I found very sad. You couldn't even make jokes about Franco's wife, who was a well-known and carefully-protected kleptomaniac. "So, Mrs. Franco, pick up anything in town?" He was having fun, so I let it go to keep good relations.

My stuff sold well at the campground, partially because I had been polishing my non-pitch sales pitch. This basically consisted of sitting at my work-table and making hippie jewelry while describing the exotic locales it came from. A backpacker from Boston would be enthralled: "Wow," she would say. "You really bought this in the middle of the *medina* in Marrakech?"

"Yeah," I would say, remembering the transaction. "The shopkeeper who sold me this one had an eye patch and a baby goat that sat on his lap. Probably enjoyed it as a pet until it became the guest of honor at a feast. He looked like a pirate who had decided to quit the seafaring life and raise livestock," all of which was entirely true. I didn't have to make up bizarre stories about what I saw in Morocco. In fact, I learned to leave out some of the most interesting stuff because people thought I was lying. People looked at me sideways, for example, when I told them about the night I got a room in Marrakech for a quarter. Twenty-five cents for lodging seems like an exaggeration, but I swear it's true. The room was on the second floor of a place that made a ghetto house look like the Taj Mahal. It had a door that didn't lock, the floor was covered with hay, and there was no electricity or running water. So it was worth about a quarter. It beat sleeping in an alley, where you could get your throat cut for your shoes. I shared it with six guys, and we all had bedrolls because we were all traveling. I was the only American. The rest were African—Sudanese, Tunisian, Nigerian. One of us had to stay there at all times to watch our stuff, so there were arguments when somebody was late for their shift. I lasted two nights and moved on to a swanky joint that cost two bucks a night.

The campground in Barcelona had an energetic contingent of Europeans and North Americans, and I happened to fall in with a group of Germans who were traveling together. There were two couples and a guy named Dieter—the designated "fifth wheel." Dieter and I just clicked right away for some reason, probably because we were the two guys without girlfriends in the group. He was from a place in Germany that other Germans made jokes about—like Mississippi in the States—so we had something in common and made each other laugh. So Dieter and I became good buddies and we'd all go out to the bars at night and do what young people do—drink too much and get rowdy and stumble home late at night and crash in our respective tents. Germans are known as serious drinkers, and this crew certainly did nothing to debunk the stereotype. They could drink twice as much as I could and still function the next day. If I drank more than three beers I'd feel like I'd been run over by an asphalt machine, so I paced myself.

Naturally, I'd get up earlier than my buddies, so when they'd stagger out of their tents at 11 a.m. or noon, I'd have been up making "jewelry" for two hours (calling me a *jeweler* was like calling a ditch-digger an *earth sculptor*. I strung beads on a leather thong and kept them in place with bronze wire twisted on with needle-nosed pliers, so I didn't deserve the title). Still, my German friends loved to look through my interesting merchandise, and they bought a ton of stuff. When they were gathered around, it would attract other campers, and Dieter enjoyed being a shill. He'd be looking at my trinkets, pretending he didn't know me, and some campers—a couple from Holland, say—would come up to see what I was selling. One of them would ask the price of a necklace and I'd say ten bucks, and Dieter would start speaking German to them and in a few minutes they'd buy a couple of pieces without trying to get my price down. The first time it happened, of course, I asked him what he said.

He'd told them a sob story about me: a partner had ripped me off, and I was unloading my goods at cost just so I could get enough cash to go home. "I told them you were a nice guy for an American, but kind of a dumb businessman. I said you didn't know this stuff was worth much more, so they shouldn't take advantage of you."

Dieter probably sold $300 worth of stuff for me while we were there, so I never let him pay for a beer. He liked the arrangement and was happy to keep playing the role. He was one of the main reasons I ran out of inventory in Barcelona and had to head back south before I even got out of Spain. Some Americans had told me about the American naval base in the town of Rota, on the southern Atlantic coast of Spain. It was only a hundred miles or so out of my way, so I thought I'd check it out. I had an idea for a bartering situation that might work in my favor. Besides, I liked the idea of having some laughs with a few guys who spoke my language. Little did I realize that doing just that would cause a military security alert, almost trigger an international incident, and nearly get me thrown into a Spanish jail.

Chapter Seven:

Borders, Blunders, and Brouhahas

I drove the length and breadth of the little sea-side town of Rota in about fifteen minutes, getting a feel for the place. The old section had been built right down to the water, and at high tide the waves slapped against the concrete retaining wall that prevented the shops from gradually getting pounded away by the sea. The fish market and little restaurants downtown were all very quaint, and there were quite a few named "streets" that were more like alleys. They were so narrow that if I drove into them with my van I'd get dirty looks from people who had to stand in doorways until I passed. I learned my lesson quickly. These folks had obviously seen enough Ugly Americans for several lifetimes.

As in most military towns, a street near the base was the "strip" that consisted primarily of bars with very un-Spanish names like "O'Brians" and "King Neptune's." I peeked into a few places that were practically deserted at five p.m., but a place called "The Hong Kong Bar" seemed popular so I went in and ordered a beer. I got into a pool game and met a few guys, and they were thrilled to meet an American close to their age who *wasn't* in the military. A guy named Pete from Louisiana felt like he'd found a countryman and literally wanted to take me home with him. Not in an *inappropriate* way. He said one of his roommates was from Occan Springs, Mississippi, a stonecrab's throw from my hometown, so I ought to come on base and meet him and have a few beers and crash on an extra cot that night. I thought this was a grand idea, since my primary mission was to make a few friends and do a little "horse-trading" with them. Enjoying some good company would be *lagniappe*.

When we walked outside, it was raining hard. We sprinted to a cab and jumped in. That's how everybody got around in Rota. You got a cab to the base, a cab to the strip, a cab to the other end of the strip, a cab to Old Town to do some *"tapa-hopping."* *Tapas* are like appetizers—little tastes of octopus, mussels, herring, smoked fish, etc.—and it was a pleasant tradition to walk around to various bars at dinnertime and have a drink and a few *tapas* instead of stopping at one place for a long dinner. You got lots of different little tastes, you saw friends, and you gradually got full and a pleasant buzz.

So we got in the cab and headed toward the base in a very heavy downpour—a "frog strangler," as my uncle used to say. Just before we got to the gate, Pete switched placcs with me, putting me on the right side of the back seat, which I found a bit odd. Then he told me to get my driver's license out. "Just flash it real quick, don't make a big deal out of it," he said. Since I was in his territory, I figured he knew what he was doing, so I played along. I noticed there were both Spanish military guards and Americans manning the checkpoint. It was hard to tell who was who, though, because the rain was pretty fierce and everybody was wearing rain gear. When we got to the checkpoint, a soldier leaned down, Pete rolled the back window partially down, quickly flashed an I.D. card as I flashed my license, and then yelled "Go ahead!" at the driver.

There was a moment of confusion because the driver was supposed to take orders from the guard, not from a sailor barking from the back seat; but when he instinctively lurched forward, the guard looked at the line of cabs gathering behind us and waved us through. Pete smiled at me and said, "Piece of cake," and I wondered if I'd been hasty in trusting this dude. The next morning, I found out in a very scary way that I had.

We had a pretty low-key evening, hoisting a few and playing Do You Know with Danny, the kid from the coast. I crashed on an extra cot, and in the morning Pete said he'd accompany me off the base. We grabbed one of the ubiquitous cabs, and just before we got to the checkpoint, Pete again gave me instructions. When I flashed my license at the guard, he immediately looked annoyed and barked, "I don't want to see your fucking driver's license, show me your I.D.!" Pete croaked, "Oh, Jesus," and all the blood left his face. I fumbled in my wallet and whispered, "What do I do? Tell me what to do!"

"Don't you have any other I.D.?" whispered Pete.

"I got my passport, do I show that? Tell me what to do!"

By this time, of course, the guard sensed trouble and ordered the driver to pull out of line and wait. Pete was terrified, almost in tears. "Oh, man," he moaned, "I'm dead, I'm dead! They write me up again and I'm dead!" Then he started begging me not to tell them it was his fault. "They won't be as rough on you," he whined.

Great. Terrific. So it's left up to me to save this jackass who got me in trouble. Thanks a lot. My mind was racing through the possibilities, but I didn't know what my options might be or what I was going to do. After a minute, the guard sent the driver away and ordered us both into the guard shack. He ordered us to sit down and not move until his superior arrived, and I knew this was serious. Pete looked like a condemned man—his lip quivered, his face was blue-white, his fingers twitched. I didn't know what his punishment would be, but I was pretty sure it was *not* staying in for recess and writing *I won't sneak unauthorized persons onto the base* a hundred times.

We sat there avoiding each other's eyes for a few minutes, and then I heard the whine of a vehicle screaming toward the guardhouse from inside the base. A jeep screeched to a stop outside the guardhouse, and before it had even stopped rocking, three very serious-looking MP's jumped out and double-timed it to the building, two of them carrying rifles. I really didn't think an execution would be necessary, but I must admit that the sight of uniformed men carrying firearms on my account and looking decidedly out of sorts was more than a little unsettling. The ranking officer among them—a bull-necked guy as short and sturdy as a speed-bump—looked at me and barked, "Is this him!?" and the guard shouted, "Yes, SIR!" Bull Neck barked at me to stand up and show him my I.D. and I immediately obliged.

He stared at my passport, back at me, then looked at Pete, who looked like he was moments from having a stroke. "Where's your I.D.?" he spat, and I knew it was time to act. I made my decision based on the hope that Pete the Chowderhead was right about one thing—that they'd be harder on him than on me. And I must admit that my ulterior motive was to ingratiate myself with a sailor who might be able to do me a favor.

As Pete was reaching for his I.D. with shaking hands, I spoke up. "Sir, this guy had nothing to do—"

"Did I say you could talk?!" screamed Bull Neck, leaning in so close to me that the hard brim of his hat chopped a crease into my forehead.

I didn't want to utter an actual word, so I shook my head and shut up.

He looked at Pete's I.D., glared at Pete, then was in my face again.

"When did you get onto this base?" he snarled.

"Last night. Sir."

"What time?"

"I think it was around 7 p.m."

"Did you come through this gate?"

"Yes, sir."

"Who let you through?"

"I can't really say for sure because it was raining and everybody was in rain gear," which was true. "I just got into town and thought I'd go on the base and talk to some Americans. I figured my passport would get me in, so I grabbed a cab. When I got here, I just raised up my passport and the guy waved us through."

"What guy? Spanish or American?"

"I-I really don't know, sir, I—"

"Did his uniform look like this or like that," he said, pointing to a guard outside.

"Like I said, he was in rain gear, so—"

A Spanish guard heard the commotion and came to investigate, and Bull Neck pointed at him. "Did his uniform look like that?"

"Sir, I wish I could tell you, but I couldn't really see a uniform, he—"

"There is a problem?" said the Spanish guard, looking annoyed.

"Yeah, there's a problem, one of your guys waved this asshole through last night, and—"

"How do you know it was one of my men?" he said, immediately testy. I got the impression these guys had a history of squabbling. They were almost shouting at each other from the start.

"You had the incoming from 1800 hours to midnight, didn't you? And I know damn well none

of my men would wave somebody through without—"

"Oh, your men don't make a mistake, eh? Like
with the woman last week."

"Don't start with that! You know goddamn
well—!"

"That is enough!" somebody yelled, and another Spanish guard came in, looking like he out-
ranked the first one. They had a quick exchange in
Spanish as the first guard spat out his contempt for
Bull Neck's attitude and stomped out of the room.
The second guard and Bull Neck then squared
off for a minute, and I started seeing ugly head-
lines: "*Mississippi Bead Merchant Triggers Span-
ish-American Hostilities.*" But the Spaniard coolly
asked Bull Neck not to be so quick to question his
men's professionalism without solid evidence, and
suggested that they have a meeting with their com-
manding officers and discuss the issue later. Bull
Neck snorted and puffed up before agreeing, and
an international incident was avoided, thank God.
Then he remembered the catalyst for the chaos and
glared at me again.

"So you flashed your passport?"

"Yes, sir. And he waved us through."

"Us? Who's us? Was this guy with you?"

"No, sir, I meant me and the cab driver. This
guy had nothing to do with anything." I looked at
Pete. "I'm sorry for dragging you into this, pal. I
didn't know there'd—"

"Did I say you could talk to him?!" he screamed,
the veins bulging like vines on his neck. "Why were
you in the same cab with him?"

"I just saw him walk out of a barracks twenty
minutes ago and asked him if he'd share a cab back
into town," I lied. "He was just doing me a favor."

Bull Neck stared at us both another moment,
then handed Pete his I.D. "Get out of here," he said,
and Pete hustled out, avoiding my eyes.

He asked me what I did on the base last night, and I lied a bunch. I said I didn't know my way around, and it was raining like crazy, so I just found a dry spot under the eaves of some kind of storage building and went to sleep. Fortunately, I looked like I'd spent the night curled up under a bush, so it was at least feasible. He looked at my passport again, then took off his hat and stepped so close to me that our chests were touching. He gritted his teeth and glared into my eyes to indicate just how serious he was about what he was saying.

"Here's what's going to happen, Mr. Dryden from Moss Point, Mississippi," he said in a scary, whispered growl. "And I want you to listen very closely because I'm just going to say it once."

I thought it was pretty obvious that he had my undivided attention, but I tried to look even more attentive than before.

"I think you're just a dumb-ass that blundered on to my base in the rain because some pansy-ass didn't want to get his uniform wet," he said, "so I'm going to let you go this time." The knot in my gut loosened a tad. Then he leaned in so close that his nose actually touched mine. "But if you ever, ever, *ever* come onto my base without the proper authorization again for any reason, or in *any* kind of weather, Mr. Dryden—I don't give a shit if a hurricane blows you in here, you understand?" I nodded. "If I catch you on my base, I'm not going to put you in our brig, I'm not going to file a report, I'm not going to worry about your sorry ass at all, Mr. Dryden. You know what I'm going to do?" I admitted with a head shake that I did not. "I'm going to give you to the Spanish police, Mr. Dryden, because you're breaking a Spanish law, too, you see. And you know what? Their jails aren't nearly as nice as ours, and they don't have the American Bill of Rights, and in fact they don't think prisoners have many rights at all and they don't give a fuck if you cry for a lawyer or your mama or the fucking President of the United States if they've got your ass in their jail. They do whatever they want to do to you. Are you getting this, Mr. Dryden? Am I coming through loud and clear?"

I nodded again.

"What did you say?"

"Yes, SIR! I understand, sir. Thank you, sir."

"Good," he said. He paused another second before he slammed my passport into my chest, knocking me back a step. "Now get the fuck off my base."

I didn't tell him that nothing in the world could make me happier than getting the fuck off his base. Fighting the urge to skip, I walked out and headed toward town.

I got a couple of blocks before I saw Pete, sulking in the shadows, looking like the hangdog chowderhead he was. He started yelling apologies when I was about forty yards away. He gave me plenty of room when I got close, aware that I had every right to punch him in the mouth, but lashing out at anybody was the last thing on my mind. I couldn't even work up a nasty grimace. I was so relieved and thankful to be free that I felt like I was floating along on a pink cloud of liberty. A couple of months later, when I broke the law in another country, my luck ran out and I desperately longed to experience that feeling again.

Naturally, Pete gushed all over me for saving his bacon, practically kissing my feet in gratitude. I had saved an important part of his life. He said he'd do anything to repay me, *anything,* so the timing seemed right. "Now that you mention it," I said, "there is this one little thing you could do."

A couple of days later, I met Pete in the Hong Kong Bar, and he had a bag of goodies for me from the PX on base. The sailors could get all kinds of stuff for a fraction of what you'd pay for it back in the States. Certain items—new designer jeans and American cigarettes, for example—were so hard to come by in Europe that they were like money on the street. He gave me six pairs of jeans and ten cartons of various American smokes, and he wouldn't take a dime. "So are we even?" he asked, still contrite. I smiled and shook his hand and told him we were.

He probably paid less than a hundred bucks for the stuff, and I had saved him from getting busted down a rank and a pay grade—a pretty darned good exchange from his point of view. And I knew that in Morocco, I could trade it for merchandise that I'd eventually turn into maybe $3,000 in profit, so I got a good deal, too. The next day, I pointed my van toward Africa.

I decided to take the van this time because the blue jeans and cigarettes were bulky to carry, and I thought I might need the space hauling stuff back. I met a couple of American guys waiting to get on the ferry, and told them I'd take them to Marrakech if they'd split gas with me. They happily accepted, thrilled to be traveling with someone who'd been before and ecstatic that we'd have our own wheels. We had no way of knowing that only one of them would make it.

On my first trip, when I got to Ceuta, I took a bus to the border and got through the checkpoint in fifteen minutes. This time I had to sit in line behind about forty vehicles, so we were there for a couple of hours at least. I found out that Bill and Richard, my twenty-something passengers, had met in Madrid and decided to travel together for awhile. We spent the time in line telling our life stories and how we happened to end up where we were. As the line inched along, we'd get out from time to time and push the van a few feet forward to conserve gas. I also used the time to stash the blue jeans and cartons of cigarettes into as many obscure nooks and crannies as possible, hiding most of the cigarettes at the bottom of a box of kitchen supplies. I told the guys to keep all their valuables—especially things that could easily disappear into someone's pocket—on their bodies, not in their gear in the van.

When we finally got to the checkpoint, it was dark. As bugs fluttered around naked light bulbs, a Moroccan guard told us to get out of the van so he could compare our faces with our passport photos. Meanwhile, as we were lined up ten yards away, another guard poked around in the van looking for contraband—and probably for small, valuable items he could slip in his pocket. The guys were thankful I had warned them. I'm not singling out Morocco as the only country with larcenous border guards, by the way. It's a universal plague I've run into from the Caribbean to Western Europe. Relatively affluent foreign travelers are easy targets who aren't in a position to make a stink.

The guard told us to stay where we were and took our passports inside the building. We stood there long enough for the guy driving the car behind ours to get impatient and ask what the hell was going on. A guard went over and—if I read his body language and tone correctly—told him to keep his *djellaba* on, they were checking out the Americans. Then they started talking about us, because this was late in 1973, when American relations with the Arab world were very volatile. Egypt and Syria had attacked Israel, the U.S. had come to Israel's aid, angering the Arabs, and OPEC stopped the flow of oil to the Land of the Free—the infamous Oil Embargo of 1973-74. The price of gas in the U.S. rose from thirty cents a gallon to more than a buck in a couple of months, fomenting anti-Arab sentiment in the U.S. and a lot of economic saber-rattling. As we stood at the border to an Arab nation, I was hoping the guards wouldn't hold all those political complications against us.

After what seemed like an hour, the guard returned. He handed Richard and me our passports and said we could proceed. He handed Bill his and said, "You, no," and motioned for him to go back to Spain. As you can imagine, the scene quickly got chaotic as Bill tried to find out why he was being denied entry, Richard yelled to him asking what he should do, and I tried to tell the guard that Bill's gear was in the van, so he'd have to at least let him get it. All this happened in about four seconds in three different languages, so there was a lot of yelling and jostling and guards started converging from every direction. Not realizing that I was making a dangerous mistake, I walked quickly toward the guard who was escorting Bill away. I hadn't gone more than three steps before a guard stepped out of a doorway, pointed a gun at my chest and barked some Arabic at me. I had no idea what he'd said and didn't care. I just immediately used the universal signal for *I promise not to do anything you'd need to shoot me for:* I raised my hands and fell to my knees. I didn't want him to think for a *second* that I had any Action Hero inclinations. It occurred to me that I probably needed to work on my checkpoint etiquette, since I had caused a lot of screaming at two in about a week.

The guy pointing the gun at me yelled Arabic at me for awhile, so I kept my hands in full view, tried to remain as still as a statue, and generally tried to give him the impression that I just could not *possibly* agree with him any more, that I *was* in fact a worthless imperialist jackal, or whatever it was he was calling me. After a moment, the guard who had inspected our passports came back and told the gun-pointer that he could aim the piece somewhere else, he'd take it from here, and I breathed for the first time in about a minute.

Things calmed down a bit, and the guard who was denying Bill entry explained to me that

William Johnson had misbehaved in Morocco and was on the list of people who weren't allowed into the country. I explained that that's a very common name in America, and that this young guy had never been there before, but it was rather like talking to a turban on a water jug. This guy was not going to be moved by my pleadings. Bill got his gear out of the van, graciously told Richard and me to have a good time, and headed back into Spain.

As we drove into the darkness of Morocco, Richard said his knees were still weak and his stomach was doing somersaults. Trying to put him at ease, I chuckled and said, "Welcome to the Third World. We'll get some chicken *tajine* (stew with green olives or apricots) and mint tea in Tétouan, that'll settle your stomach." I didn't want him to know that my knees and guts felt exactly the same way, maybe worse. Seeing the muzzle of a loaded gun up close has always had that effect on me.

Having a traveling partner was a welcome change. Richard was an Italian kid from Philadelphia, so we enjoyed our background differences and made fun of each other's accents. He had a good sense of humor, but he never really seemed to relax completely after the incident at the border. That was understandable, of course. Having armed guards yelling at you in Arabic is unsettling. We slept in the van, or in dinky inns with no running water in the room and only "squat" toilets—holes in the floor with nothing to sit on. Richard grew up in the city, hadn't spent much time in the woods and had never been camping. I grew up in Mississippi and had camped all my life, so roughing it was a lot easier for me. I had probably used about the same number of bushes as bathrooms. I'll also eat damn near anything, and Richard had a harder time finding something he wanted to eat in Morocco. And for guys who looked as foreign as we did, just getting through the day in such a relatively primitive place was a challenge. Every time an aggressive street hustler approached us, Richard looked like he was being bludgeoned, while I tended to take it in stride. I had a feeling the days of our partnership were numbered.

We headed south to the dusty little town of Ouezzane, then to the famous Roman ruins of Volubilis, the best-preserved and most magnificent archeological site in the country. We marveled at the amazing mosaics and monuments, many of them dating to the Third Century A.D. I've always gotten a peculiar little thrill knowing I was touching structures that were built and used by sophisticated people many centuries before.

We headed west to Kenitra on the coast, which had been a port and trading center for centuries. So I thought it was appropriate that while we were there, I would trade a carton of Winstons for a full tank of gas. Just a couple of hours further south, we came to the sprawling nation's capitol, Rabat. We happened to stop at a little place near the train station for lunch, and I got the map out while we ate. Richard was unpleasantly surprised to see that almost 200 miles of Morocco and countless Moroccans were still between us and Marrakech, way down south. While I saw it as just another leg of a fascinating adventure, I could tell that Richard saw it as 200 miles of suspect food and hassles that would only get us deeper into this strange, un-Westernized, Burger-King-less country. He told me he wanted to check something out and walked over to the train station. I had a pretty good idea why.

When he came back fifteen minutes later, he had a ticket to Tangiers. He said he was sorry, but he'd seen enough of Morocco and wanted to get back to civilization. I understood completely and wished him luck. I helped him gather his gear from the van and walked him over to the station. "By the way," I told him, "there's a Ramada Inn about five blocks from the station in Tangiers."

"Really?" he said, and the delight and relief that brightened his face made me laugh out loud.

"Yeah," I said. "Have a cheeseburger and soak in the tub a few minutes for me, too."

He laughed and said he would, we exchanged addresses and said our goodbyes. Settling into my sleeping bag in the van that night, I had to admit it was kind of nice to have my space back. I got up at first light and headed south.

*   *   *

The road to Marrakech was pretty good, but it was two-lane all the way so anything from a flock of sheep to a rockslide could slow your progress. I was in no huge hurry, so I stopped in villages along the way to buy produce and explore. The people out in the sticks didn't have "street smarts" and weren't hardened like their city cousins, so it was a nice change of pace to buy an orange without having to haggle, and have shy little kids follow me around, daring one another to talk to me or even touch me. The merchants weren't aggressive because they didn't get many tourists to practice their spiels or scams on. They were honest, hard-working folks, just like you'd find in a town of 400 in Indiana or Kansas. I knew things would change abruptly when I hit the big city.

When I rolled into Marrakech and parked, about ten little boys surrounded me, clamoring to be my guide. I had Dutch plates on the van, so most of them were using their Dutch or German words. I wanted to get the feel of the place before I started doing business, so I told them no thanks and headed for the *Place Jemaa al-Fna*, the most famous city center in the country. I bought sizzling lamb kabobs and corn on the cob at the food kiosks, I watched fire-eaters, acrobats, and snake charmers doing their shows. I watched a man reading to a crowd of people who were as excited and transfixed as if they were watching an action movie on a big screen in living color. I watched scribes sit on blankets and read letters to illiterate families, then write their responses in that beautiful, flowing script.

I explored the *souq* pretty thoroughly, asking questions and checking out what was available. I noticed that a few street vendors had blue jeans, but most of them were cheap knock-offs. The few who had genuine Levis or Wranglers were wearing expensive clothes and flashy jewelry themselves, so they were obviously in a higher trading bracket. I asked a few tobacconists if they had any American cigarettes. Most didn't, and the few who did retrieved them from secure hiding places and wanted major money for them. My barter situation was looking good.

I had a pretty good feel for the place by nightfall, so I walked back to the van and found a safe place to sleep a couple of miles out of town.

The next morning I decided it was time to start doing some business. I drove back to where the youthful guides had rushed me before, and they appeared right on cue. When they started jabbering in Dutch and German, I yelled, "I'm an American!" and the response was comical. Imagine a dozen ten-year-old Arab boys all trying to out-American each other: "Whatcha lookin' for, man? Where you from, East Coast? California? What's happenin'? You a Yankee fan? Anything you want, man, I know where to find it!"

I picked a bright-looking kid from the gaggle and asked him a couple of questions to see if he could actually speak English. He couldn't—the street kids just knew enough to sell a foreigner something—but he knew enough English and French that I knew we'd be able to communicate.

So I showed him one of the familiar beads and told him that's what I was looking for. He nodded vigorously and said he knew exactly where to go. I had already stuffed some jeans and cigarettes into my pack, so we headed deep into the *medina.*

If you can picture a pile of cooked spaghetti, you'll have a pretty good idea of what a map of the *medina* in Marrakech must look like. After five minutes of walking, we could have been in Borneo for all I knew. Finally, we stopped at a fabric shop that happened to be owned by a cousin of his. After some initial confusion, I told his cousin that, regrettably, I wasn't interested in buying fabric, I was looking for beads, and we took off again for Parts Unknown.

After another circuitous hike, we stopped at a pottery shop. There, I sadly had to inform his uncle I wasn't buying pots, that I was looking for beads, and that I might have to hire another guide. The man and his nephew then had a loud and dramatic exchange with lots of gesturing before my guide trotted off down the alley, waving for me to follow him. We hadn't gone very far before he stopped at a rug shop and said hello to yet another cousin, who offered us tea. My guide said, Sure, we'd love some tea, and sat down. I bowed to the man and thanked him for his hospitality, but said I don't have time for tea because I have to find another guide, and started walking away like I knew exactly where I was going. My guide chased me down, begging me for another chance, which I was counting on since I didn't have the slightest idea where I was going. I told him sorry, but I had to find a guide who didn't have so many relatives in the retail business. He started grinning and shaking his head and walking sideways along beside me, begging me to give him another chance and telling me that I had already met all his relatives who owned shops. I grabbed him by the shoulders and got his full attention. "If you take me to another shop that doesn't have any beads, I will find another guide. Do you understand?" Yes, he said, he understood perfectly, and the next place he showed me actually had some beads.

We went to several shops that had fairly piti-ful collections of what I was looking for. At first the merchants tried to sell me a necklace or a bracelet, or even a single, *very* special bead. After I explained that I wanted to buy dozens or even hundreds of beads, most of them shrugged their shoulders and pointed at what was on display. One shopkeeper grabbed a handful and put them on a scale, but I explained that I'd have to pick out each one. This seemed strange to him, but he agreed to let me sit on the floor in his shop and pick through a shoebox-sized pile of beads. After culling them for fifteen min-utes, I only had about a dozen beads. We haggled and I bought them, but I told my young guide that this was no good—I needed to find a place with *lots* of beads. He nodded that he understood and set off at a fast clip. I stayed close on his heels, because if I lost him it could take me days to find my way out of the maze. After a frantic few minutes of dodging people, sliding past donkeys, and ricocheting off pushcarts, I was infuriated to see his uncle stand-ing in his pottery shop with a wide grin, hopeful that I had changed my mind about not needing any pots. I muttered a few choice English words and stomped off to find another guide, but the shop-keeper stopped me and told me in broken French that he knew a place with *lots* of beads, *mountains* and *rivers* of beads, so many beads it would make my eyeballs spin—or something to that effect—and that he was going to tell his nephew how to take me there.

I simmered down and waited as the uncle gave the boy directions. Finding anything in a Moroc-can *medina* is kind of like finding your way around inside an ant hill—or what I imagine it to be like, anyway. I watched the boy nodding uncertainly, his brows bunched together in concentration, as his uncle tried to explain where this place was. He obviously wasn't getting it. After a few minutes, the shopkeeper threw up his hands and barked at the boy to stay there. He yelled something to the keeper of the shop next door, who yelled back that he'd watch his place for him, and we hustled into the teeming maze.

I assumed we were taking the shortest route, but we could have gone down the same alley three times and I'd never have known it. For ten minutes we hurried past ancient whitewashed walls, hundreds of doorways, and shops selling everything from tin cans to cow's tongues to fabric, charcoal, hammers, wire, and incense. It became a blur, and then we stopped at a little shop where a fat man in a *djellaba* sat on a stool in the doorway smoking roll-your-own cigarettes that had a sweetly illegal scent to them. Uncle Guide motioned that this was the place, and I tried to give him a couple of *dirham,* but he refused them and muttered something about his knuckleheaded nephew wasting my time. The other shopkeeper—let's call him Azzouzj—thanked him for bringing me to him, and then they had a little chuckle, no doubt at the expense of the naïve American.

He invited me in and I looked at a few trays of beads. I saw a few nice ones, but told him I wanted to buy at least three times that many. He crooked his finger, and I followed him as he went behind a curtain into a back room. In the dim light, I thought I saw a little round table with beads piled on top. When my eyes adjusted, I realized I was looking at a barrel overflowing with beads. I saw pots full of beads, bowls and sacks and boxes and strings of beads. I was reminded of one of those cartoon images of a pirate's treasure cave. I had found the Super Wal-Mart of African trade beads, except that none of the merchandise was new, and some pieces were centuries old. They were of every imaginable type and in various conditions: old, ancient, long, short, perfect, beat-up, beautiful, ugly, scarred, nicked, dirty, spotless and worn at the edges.

Azzouzj asked if I'd like to buy a few scoops from this basket or that pot, and I explained to him that I intended to carefully choose each and every bead that I bought. It was apparent that he thought I was a little nuts—kind of like sitting down and inspecting every pea before you buy a pound—but he shrugged and said I could stay as long as I wanted.

I sat on the floor and sifted through baskets, fascinated by the craftsmanship and beauty of the beads. I knew that the finer the specimens I found, the easier they would be to sell, so I took my time. I started several piles: big whole ones, little whole ones, big imperfect ones, little ones that matched, big ones with an end missing, etc. A "big" one was about the size of my forefinger, and some were as small as a pencil eraser. As I sat on the floor culling beads, customers and acquaintances of the shopkeeper would occasionally stop by, and Azzouzj would have to tell them the story of the slightly wacky American every time. He had it down to shorthand after about four visitors.

I had been culling for half an hour when I reached in my knapsack and pulled out a pack of cigarettes. I asked Azzouzj if he had children, and when he turned in his chair to answer me, I casually opened the brand-new pack of Marlboros, tapped one out and lit it. I saw his eyes lock on the famous red-and-white pack like lasers, then look away as if he hadn't noticed. When I was in Morocco, most of the tobacco available to the average guy was harsh Turkish "black" tobacco, and the cheaper stuff even had hard little twig-like stems—kind of like yard clippings—mixed in with the tobacco. The so-called "blonde" or Virginia tobacco used in most American brands was highly prized for its smoothness, uniformity and taste. I offered him a cigarette, and he accepted it oh-so-casually as if he were offered a Marlboro every day. He smoked, and—not being a smoker—I pretended to, while he told me about his family. About that time an acquaintance of his stopped by, and when his eyes hungrily locked onto the Marlboros, I offered him one and he gratefully accepted.

The two of them smoked and chatted, and the acquaintance was obviously very impressed that Azzouzj had a Western customer in his shop giving him American cigarettes. After a couple more friends happened by and were given Marlboros, a fairly steady stream of visitors happened to be in the neighborhood and dropped by to say hello—some of them twice. I gave them all cigarettes, which they accepted with deep gratitude, touching their lips and their hearts in the Moroccan way. I put the pack on a stool near my host and welcomed him to smoke as many as he liked, and Azzouzj was very grateful for the gesture.

One of the men who stopped by for a smoke was wearing some fairly cheap designer jeans. I complimented him on them and asked him if he had bought them in Marrakech. He said yes, but that they were very expensive, rubbing his fingers together to make the point. I said, "Maybe you can help me. Do you know anyone who'd be interested in buying these?" and I pulled out a pair of Levis with the tags still attached.

I had surprised him, so before he could control his reaction, his eyes widened and he whispered the Arabic equivalent of "Good God in Heaven, would you look at that?!" and even reached out to feel the sturdy fabric. He quickly pulled his hand back and tried to recover, but his poker face had crumbled beyond repair. He shrugged, grimaced, and yawned, trying to look bored, as if he saw factory-fresh Levis every other day, and said he might be able to find somebody to give me a few dirham for them.

"Try two hundred," I said with a smile, and Azzouzj almost gagged. Two hundred dirham was about $50, an exorbitant sum for a pair of pants in 1973. Azzouzj picked them up for a closer look and the two of them had a quick, furtive conversation that I'm sure went something like this:

"Is the American crazy? Two hundred dirham for a pair of blue jeans?!"

"He's not crazy, they get twice that for real Levis in Casablanca."

"How much could you get for them here?"

"At least a hundred and fifty, maybe two."

"Holy mother of Mohammed."

"Truly. There are people who would kill for these."

"You think I should try to buy them from him?"

"If you don't, I will. I know ten guys who'd give you cash or hashish for them right now."

While they were having their not-so-discreet conversation, another smoker who had heard about the Marlboros stopped by, saw the Levis on Azzouzj's lap and blurted the equivalent of "Sweet Shivering Sheherazade, Azzouzj! Where'd you get the Levis!?" and everybody's cover was blown. I offered him a cigarette. "A real American cigarette?!" he enthused. "It is so rare as gold! Thank you, my friend!"

Azzouzj rolled his eyes. He knew I was in trading mode, and this wide-eyed yahoo wasn't helping his cause.

Over the next couple of hours, as I doled out another pack of cigarettes to Azzouzj's appreciative acquaintances, I gleaned what I deemed a fairly wondrous collection of beads from the mountains of chaff—about three shoeboxes full—and put them in four baskets. I figured a Moroccan would probably pay in the neighborhood of $80 to $100 for them, so I was prepared to trade about twice that much in goods. I told Azzouzj I had found what I wanted, and gave him an unopened pack of Marlboros as a little token of my appreciation for letting me spend most of the day in his shop. Little gifts softened the bargaining process considerably, I had found. He thanked me, then yelled down the alley and a 12-year-old boy materialized. He gave the boy instructions and a handful of dirham, and he trotted off into the darkening *medina.*

I opened negotiations by offering him the Levis and the remaining eight packs in the carton of Marlboros. Azzouzj countered by pushing two of the baskets aside and asking for three more packs of cigarettes. It was obvious that he'd be shooting for the moon, so I was glad I was bargaining with goods that had cost me nothing.

The boy came back with a delicious spread of grilled meats and vegetables, so we took a break to eat. As a courtesy, I offered to pay, and my host of course declined. After more haggling, we finally agreed on a trade. As I recall, he ended up with three pairs of jeans and three or four cartons of cigarettes—probably five times what the beads were worth—so he was thrilled and I was quite satisfied. At the rate I sold beads, I figured I had two months worth of inventory, about all I wanted to carry.

By this time, it was almost dark. Now that the word was out that I had *American Gold* on my person, I didn't like the idea of having a mere boy accompany me back to my van at night. I asked Azzouzj if he knew of a man who would escort me for a pack of cigarettes. His face split into a brown-toothed grin and said he knew of at least twenty, how many did I need? I said, "One big one, or two little ones," and we had a good laugh. He yelled into the alley, the same boy materialized, got instructions, and returned ten minutes later with two guys about my size.

Azzouzj and I said our thanks and goodbyes. One of the guys picked up my pack, and my security detail and I headed into the dark maze, which was now an exotic wonderland of glowing windows, fragrant wood smoke, dinnertime aromas and candlelight. The fellow carrying my pack led the way, and the other man stayed in actual physical contact with me most of the way, guiding me around corners and over obstacles, gently wedging a path for me through clusters of people. I felt like The Great White Hunter being led through darkest Africa by friendly natives.

When we got to the van, I stashed the pack safely inside and handed them each a pack of cigarettes. They bowed and scraped, wished me *bon chance,* and melted back into the darkness. I headed out of town to look for the same place I had camped without incident the night before.

When I awoke the next morning a few kilometers north of town, I prepared to return to Marrakech as a tourist just to experience that ancient, fascinating city. Then I realized that I had made a strategic mistake, and the more I thought, the more paranoid I got. Too many people knew I had valuable goods in my possession, and the van was pretty vulnerable. I wondered if there were secure lockers at the train station, or maybe a hotel where I could stash the stuff for the price of a good tip. But I would still have to carry my pack through unfamiliar territory and bring it back to the van. I finally decided I wouldn't be able to relax enough to enjoy the city, so I headed north.

The trip went smoothly until I had the aforementioned flat tire in Meknès and got scammed by the larcenous tire repair man. Of course, that led to the wonderful meal with the country mechanic and his gorgeous little family, so in the end I was glad I had gotten ripped off. After that memorable visit, I made good time to Ceuta and rolled onto the ferry to Spain.

*   *   *

I had spent a fair amount of time in Spain, so I decided to just make a beeline for France and not worry about making any money along the way. I had a pretty good grubstake from my run up the Costa Blanca and I felt pretty secure with the goods I had, so I thought this might be a good time to pay my respects to the City of Light.

Paris was as amazing as I had hoped, and I made the required pilgrimages: The Eiffel Tower, the *Louvre* and smaller jewels of museums, The *Arc de Triomphe,* a stroll through *Montmartre,* coffee and *croissants* at a sidewalk café. But I was also a merchant in a peculiar business, so naturally I have a wild tale of plying my trade in Paris. Since I would eventually find myself in a dreary foreign jail, it was kind of ironic that in Paris I broke a law along with forty other outlaws, and I was one of the few who didn't get arrested.

I was there in September, I believe, so all the foreign students were back in school. The only campground I could find was inhabited primarily by retirees and families, folks who weren't interested in my beads at all. But as I made my rounds of the landmarks, I saw literally hundreds of young African immigrants selling trinkets from their native lands. Dozens of them would spread their blankets in the shadow of the Eiffel tower and coax tourists to buy ivory and wood carvings, silver bracelets, little purses, toe-rings—all kinds of exotic goods from the Dark Continent. I saw policemen walking within a few dozen yards of these street vendors, and they didn't seem to pay them any undue attention, so I thought I'd give it a try.

On my first trip to the *Louvre,* when I went strictly as a tourist, I had walked through an entrance tunnel about fifty yards long that was lined on both sides, blanket to blanket, with around forty of these African street peddlers. That seemed like a good place to start, so a few days later I put a small blanket and some of my latest creations in my knapsack, grabbed my handy Tourist Guide of Paris and a snack, and took the Metro to the *Louvre*. As before, the tunnel was lined on both sides with the peddlers. After a little searching I finally found a spot, and the guys on both sides cordially made a little room for me. I arranged my beads on the blanket and sat back hoping someone would stop. A few tourists did stop, and I sold a couple of pieces.

I had been there about an hour when suddenly all hell broke loose. A chain reaction started at the mouth of the tunnel when the guys at that end erupted in panic, frantically wrapping their blankets around their merchandise and running like hell. As the others saw what was happening, they started grabbing up their stuff and sprinting out the other end of the tunnel, dropping bracelets and little carved elephants and trinkets all over the place.

I didn't know for sure what was happening, but it was obvious that it would not be a *good* thing for people selling trinkets on blankets, which of course included me. Realizing I had an innate advantage over the coal-black Sub-Saharans who were scattering willy-nilly, I quickly stuffed my blanket and beads into my knapsack, pulled out an apple and the fold-out map from my Tourist Guide, and leaned back on my knapsack studying the map and chewing fruit.

At that moment a phalanx of Parisian policemen rushed into the tunnel, grabbing peddlers and dragging them to a paddy wagon, and another contingent that had covered the rear escape route were grabbing people on that end. In the middle of the chaos, an officer rushed at me, saw a white guy holding a Tourist Guide, munching on an apple, and looking stunned by the police action swirling around him. I obviously didn't fit the profile, so he moved on.

Meanwhile, the pincer tactic was working well for the police, and my guess is that ninety percent of the peddlers were arrested. Innocent visitors to the museum were caught in the middle of the chaos, of course, and I was treated to a comical scene that unfolded right in front of me. One of the peddlers, in a desperate last-ditch effort to escape, fell into step with a group of tourists who were obviously traveling together. Unfortunately for the African, they were Nordic types with alabaster skin, blonde hair and blue eyes, and he was pitch-black and about six inches taller than all of them. He looked as out of place as a giraffe with a bunch of penguins. A policeman spotted him, and they had a Marx Brothers moment: The policeman looked at him and shrugged, meaning, "Come on, pal, who are you trying to kid?" The African responded with a shrug of his own, meaning, "Hey, I had to give it a shot." He held out his wrists and the cop handcuffed him.

I suppose the police scheduled raids every once in awhile to remind the peddlers that they were breaking the law and to keep them from completely taking over the city. Legitimate shop owners no doubt complained bitterly about lax enforcement. In smaller numbers, they added color to the street scene. Left unchecked, they would have turned the City of Light into the City of Dark Men on Blankets. In any case, I was relieved to have escaped the round-up.

Since the campgrounds were empty of students, I had to change my business plan. I looked for funky little shops that catered to the hippie crowd, and did fairly well selling a dozen or so pieces at a time. After I had seen the sights and visited all the likely shops I could find, it was time to move on. I toured the French countryside, visiting cities along the way—Boulogne, Reims, Calais, Lyon, Toulouse, Marseilles—and found at least one shop in every city that wanted to display some African trade beads.

By December, it was time for another buying trip to Morocco, and I looked forward to it for a couple of reasons. For one thing, the frigid nights in the van were getting uncomfortable, so I looked forward to the slightly warmer climate. And I had to admit that Morocco had cast a strange spell on me. I missed the slower pace, the simpler existence, and the constant fascination of being in a totally alien environment. Had I known a jail term awaited me, I'd have stayed awhile longer in the Western world.

Chapter Eight:

Bad Timing for Temporary Insanity

I left the van in Algeciras and decided to head to Fez, where I found the last person to blame for my jail term and slugged him in the mouth.

Actually, there were quite a few blameworthy folks—street hustlers, shopkeepers and thieves from Tangiers to Marrakech whom I would be remiss not to mention. I caught a seventy-year-old woman walking off with my shoes one day when I awoke from a nap in the country. When I chased and stopped her she was just *shocked* that the shoes belonged to me: "I am *soooo* sorry," she babbled, "I thought someone just left them there." Right, Granny. I just happened to park in the middle of nowhere beside a nice pair of Trekkers.

That was another reason I chose to leave the van in Spain on my next buying trip: it attracted scavengers and opportunists.

I got on the ferry to Ceuta on a blustery February day, glad to have my poncho between me and the cold drizzle. I took the train down to the ancient city of Fez. Although it is rich in historical treasures, Fez isn't quite as popular a tourist destination as Marrakech. My plan was to visit a few noteworthy landmarks, then find some shops deep in the *medina* where the trade beads hadn't been picked over too badly. Many of the complex systems of alleys and footpaths in ancient African towns were intentionally designed like mazes to confuse invaders, and they still work beautifully on American visitors in the 20th century. Nothing can make a resourceful, college-educated explorer feel stupider than being lost in a town designed by ancient illiterates. Fortunately, I was rarely in a hurry and didn't mind getting lost. I could always find a boy who, for about a quarter, would happily lead me to a landmark I knew.

I found a cheap room, stashed my stuff and headed out to the *souq*. The day was clear and cool, and I was glad I had dressed warmly when I got into the narrow alleyways that rarely get direct sunlight.

I was ambling aimlessly, rather enjoying being thoroughly lost, when a gold-toothed, rat-faced slime-ball slithered up beside me and grabbed my arm while saying "Good morning, my friend" in German, Dutch, and finally English. I instinctively recoiled, pulled away from him and assumed a defensive posture. He was wearing sunglasses and Western clothes—standard issue for a street hustler who mistakenly thought Westerners would be disarmed by his accouterments. He smiled broadly and shrugged, his gold teeth gleaming shark-like between his thin Sheriff of Nottingham goatee and mustache. When I pulled away, I blurted, "What the hell—?" inadvertently breaking down the language barrier.

"Ah, you American? English?" he said, wedging his rat snout into the opening. "I got best leather in Fez, best prices, you come down this way." He pointed into—literally—a dark alley. "You look, I give you good deal. Best prices anywhere in Fez. I show you, come."

By this time I had spent a total of about eight weeks in Morocco on three purchasing trips and had learned to stay on high alert and keep my radar active. I looked around quickly and saw another guy wearing sunglasses who suddenly busied himself looking at some fabric in a shop. He was obviously working with Ratface, but I didn't know their game. I happened to glance at the owner of the fabric shop— a big, bearded teddy-bear of a guy in the traditional *burnouse* or cloak—and he was clearly annoyed that these jokers were anywhere near his shop. I didn't know exactly what Ratface and his buddy had in mind for me. I just knew that shopkeepers usually didn't touch me, and they were usually inside their shops or only steps away. I didn't like his aggressive style, and I sure as hell wasn't going anywhere with him. I said, *"Merci, non,"* (*No thanks*) and started walking away. He grabbed me a second time and I felt the blood rush to my face and that Little Insane Guy inside my head start to hyperventilate.

I used all the self-control I could muster to un-clench my fists, take a breath, and cool down. The middle of a *medina* in the middle of a Third World country would be a bad place to let the Little Insane Guy lose his cool.

I closed my eyes and thought, "What we have here is a failure to communicate." A word of expla-nation about that: Morocco was a French protec-torate for the first half of the 20th century, so most Moroccans under the age of forty or so spoke pretty fluent French, which is primarily how I communi-cated, since I had minored in it and picked up a lot more in France. But, of course, the hustlers and shopkeepers had to know bits of English, Dutch and German to make sales. Some of them were virtuosos. I was walking through the *souq* in Mar-rakech one day when someone said very clearly, "You'n Amurican?" in a distinctively Texas accent. I whipped around looking for a fellow countryman and found a twelve-year-old Moroccan boy grinning at me. He had shadowed a Texan long enough to do a perfect imitation, and he used it like a lasso. I let the talented Urchin Impressionist lead me to a shop where I ended up buying some shirts.

I wasn't as charmed by Ratface. In slow motion, I used a basic self-defense move to remove his hand from my elbow. I turned and looked him in the face. "*La*," I said (*No*), and walked away the third time.

I had learned a few phrases in Arabic, the most common language in the cities, because the natives found it amusing and charming when I said *yes, no, hello, goodbye, thank you,* and counted in their melodic language. I also learned a few phrases that came in handy in certain situations, all of which I used when he grabbed me the *third* time. I knocked away his hand and spit in Arabic, "I'm not interested, leave me alone," and finally, "Touch me again and I'll knock your head off."

I turned and was trying to make my getaway when I heard him say something in Arabic before he rushed up behind me and grabbed me a *fourth* time, this time in a decidedly unfriendly way. When he spun me around, I shoved him in the chest. He stumbled backwards a few steps before he lost his balance and sprawled in the dust. I saw his henchman take a step toward me, so I bared my teeth, pointed at his chest and shouted, "*La!*" He turned kind of pale and backed up a step. I could tell he didn't really want to get any boo-boos on his skull for a couple of lousy dirham.

Meanwhile, Ratface had regained verticality and was spitting with rage—probably because a dozen people in the nearby shops had seen him bounce on his butt. He growled and charged me.

I very easily could have side-stepped him and fended off his attacks with "soft" defensive maneuvers. I could have even raised my hands and in diplomatic French or Arabic or even English said something approximating "Wait! Let's not do this! Fighting is silly! Let's be friends!" But, unfortunately, the Little Insane Guy overrode my logic control and my emotions took over.

I hit him. Okay, that's kind of an understatement. I actually hit him for quite awhile. Because by that time I was as furious as he was. He was bullying me, grabbing me, *denying me my freedom,* and I was just by God *sick* of him and every other street hustler who had tried to rip me off in those scattered eight weeks. But of course every other street hustler wasn't there, just Ratface, and he was running at me, snarling, with his gold teeth bared, not knowing he was about to pay for the sins of a couple hundred of his countrymen.

Unfortunately for Ratface, he was acting on instinct and rage alone, and I was acting on rage and four years of training in *tae kwon do*. I was twenty-four and as fast and strong as I'd ever be. He was a wiry guy, about 150 pounds, built kind of like me, so he probably thought he was moving pretty fast when he charged me. But compared to the guys I had fought in tournaments for four years, he looked like he was running under water. His face looked like a beach ball with gold teeth floating at me in slow motion, so I plowed a solid reverse punch—kind of a right jab from the heels—into his snout as hard as I could. He staggered sideways, his wrap-arounds dangling off of one ear, his nose already bleeding, trying to find me with watery eyes that were temporarily looking in different directions.

I whipped around to make sure his henchman wasn't going to jump me, but he was backing away turning a whiter shade of pale. Apparently the standard fair-haired blue-eyed tourists he was accustomed to ripping off were of a more reserved nature. I bared my teeth at him, lunged forward and barked like a dog—the universal language of wackos. Not surprisingly, he took off like a scalded greyhound, probably losing standing in the Henchman's Union.

Sensing a group of shopkeepers and passersby watching the melee, I glanced around quickly to see if I could spot anybody likely to jump a foreign devil to help defend a countryman. I saw no likely threats, just ordinary peace-loving citizens who couldn't turn away from such a spectacle but had no intention of participating. Ratface was on his own.

He put his hand to his face, saw blood on his fingers, focused on me, and made a serious error in judgment: he charged again.

That was when I made the same error I made when Chuck Norris kicked my butt across a Texas gymnasium. I allowed the Little Insane Guy to completely neutralize any sense of judgment I had left. I wasn't a rational being anymore. I was an animal, poked and prodded and attacked, and my brain shut down as my animal instincts took over. I attacked him with a pent-up ferocity I didn't know was in me. I hit him with my fists, my feet and my elbows as he flailed helplessly and the onlookers screamed at me to stop. I remember one gray-bearded man being brave enough to reach in and grab my arm, pleading with me, but I jerked away from him and continued hitting a beaten man trying to crawl away, blinded by blood pooling in his sockets. I vaguely remember thinking, "He's still conscious. I have to knock him out," when *WHAM!* I was slammed violently to the ground.

Although it felt like a cow had been dropped on me, I assumed a 300-pound friend of Ratface's—or maybe a rugby team—had intervened. Then my hands were cuffed behind me and I was slammed against a wall by three soldiers or policemen—I never knew which—one of whom pointed an automatic weapon at my face. He needn't have bothered. Being tackled by half the police force had knocked most of the fight out of me, and looking into the muzzle of a gun drained the rest. I knew I was in serious trouble. I bowed my head contritely and became a model of cooperation. My every move was calculated to relax the trigger finger of the guy with the gun.

I honestly don't remember how I got to the jail. We could have walked, they could have put me on a wagon or a donkey's back—that phase is a total blank because my mind contorted with horrible possibilities. Would they put me in a dungeon, shoot me, hang me? My immediate future was a sickening black unknown, because I didn't have the sense to get in trouble with the law in a *democracy*. Nooooo. I had to annoy the authorities in a *hereditary monarchy*. They don't have a Bill of Rights or the Miranda Law or the right to Johnny Cochran or *habeas corpus* or a Constitution as we know it. They have a king who is universally loved or else. His son won't have to run any campaign ads to inherit the throne. And as a foreign trouble-maker, I assumed I would have even fewer rights than the average Ahjmed on the street. They could throw me in a dungeon and feed me fish heads for the rest of my life—which might only be a couple of months under those conditions. I saw people *selling* fish heads, so I could only imagine what they fed prisoners. I didn't have to imagine for long.

Not only was my judgment off when I lost my temper, but my timing was bad. I went to jail on a Friday morning, and the wheels of justice don't move at all on the weekends. So for the first three days, I wasn't even on the books. They didn't care if I had any "priors" or even what my name was. I was just a "European" in a cell.

At the jail, they took my passport and all my valuables, of course. I assumed I'd never see my money and pocketknife again, but I was hoping I'd at least get my passport and leather belt back. I was put into a 20-by-20-foot concrete cubicle with no furniture or windows and a single naked light bulb dangling from the ceiling.

There were six or seven men in the cell when I

got there, and—having grown up watching American movies—I fully expected the Alpha Male to swagger over to me with a menacing grin and say the Arabic equivalent of "Well, looky here, boys! A tender young American! Just in time for my back rub!"

I was relieved that my arrival was unmemorable. The poor guys in that cell were feeling as whipped and lousy as I was about being there, so nobody was swaggering or grinning. We talked, of course. There were two or three who spoke French and three or four who didn't, so I would say something and it would be translated. I told them I was an American, and a couple of the younger guys demonstrated their worldliness: "New York? Chee-cago? Colee-fornia?" Nobody had heard of Mississippi. They wanted to know why I was there, so I told them I had had a fistfight with a guy who tried to rob me. They clucked their tongues sympathetically. A man about fifty scooted closer to me and gestured that he wanted to see my hands. I held them out, he took them in his, looked at them closely, sucked in his breath and started jabbering excitedly in Arabic. Suddenly it was Show and Tell, and since my hands had been *his* discovery, he supervised the exhibit, hiding my hands inside the sleeves of his *djellaba*, and yelling at the others to stop grabbing and pushing or he by God wouldn't let anybody see *anything*. Funny how people try to control *anything* when all real control has been ripped away from them. After everyone had seen the scrapes and dried blood on my hands, the consensus seemed to be that I was telling the truth. They all assured me I'd be out in no time, which made me feel a little better. I asked them why *they* were there, and—amazingly—they'd all just been minding their own business, there was a "misunderstanding" of some kind, and they got thrown in the slammer. I never got one Moroccan to admit that he'd committed an infraction of any kind. Misunderstandings, however, were quite common.

The minutes oozed by like asphalt melting. We had no way of knowing what time of day or night it was because there were no windows and the naked bulb high above us glowed relentlessly. I knew night was falling only because it got colder. There was no heat in that damp concrete box, and when the sun went down, the temperature dropped into the forties. Some of the men had been arrested in light clothing and were suffering. Someone asked the guard for blankets, and—surprisingly—we were given three or four dark brown ones with frayed edges. There was no fighting over them. One went to an older man who appeared to be in frail health, another to a skinny kid about sixteen who looked on the verge of a nervous breakdown. Four men shared the other two and even spooned for warmth. I was layered, thankfully, with a tee shirt, flannel shirt and sweater over my jeans; but I was still chattering. Gradually, we all lay down and tried to find a comfortable position to sleep on the cold, bare concrete. In case you're wondering, there is no position that's comfortable on cold, bare concrete. You curl up on your right side and lay your head on your arms until your right side is numb, then you turn over and repeat. I caught a few snatches of sleep, but a couple of the guys snored like jackhammers. Maybe for them four walls and roof was a step up.

For long, miserable hours I shivered and squirmed, my exterior tortured by the cold, my heart frozen in the grip of fear. The fear of the unknown in such an alien place was crippling. I lay there and told myself to take it one minute at a time, stay alert, and keep my eyes open even when I had them shut. And of course I asked God for forgiveness for beating one of his creatures bloody, and to please keep an eye on me.

After I had tossed and shivered for hours, a youngish guy pretended to roll in my direction accidentally and I didn't kick him away. That en-

Controlling my fears and stresses was pretty much a full-time job

couraged him to insinuate himself even closer, and before I knew it we were spooning. I never thought I'd be thankful to have a Moroccan thug to cuddle with. At least half of me was warm enough to allow the rest of me to nap. Still, that night crawled by like a turtle in molasses.

I don't know how anybody knew it was morning, but everybody started to stir at about the same time. The light hadn't changed one black iota. The weak white light from the bulb was constant, and the color of the concrete didn't change. No roosters crowed, and not because we were in a city—if I could hear a rooster, everybody could hear it, and there weren't fences high or strong enough to protect such a prize.

Breakfast was a piece of coarse bread and a cup of cool water. Lunch, however, was piece of coarse bread and a cup of slightly warmer water. Dinner was a magnificent feast of coarse bread and a cup of carefully aged water. I let it breathe a little.

When I was arrested on Friday morning there were only about half a dozen of us in the cell, but by late Saturday night there were twenty-six of us packed into that concrete chamber. Apparently a "Misunderstanding Wave" was plaguing the city. I remember the number because counting took my mind off where I was for a few minutes, and there weren't too many countable objects available. Besides, I knew I'd tell the story one day.

Most prisoners were quiet or even friendly, so the dynamic in the cell changed abruptly when two belligerent types were brought in together. They both looked like career thugs familiar with the jail drill. We knew they were trouble as soon as they told a couple of men to move and sat in the vacated spots. They slowly looked us all over, and some of the guys actually tried to disappear from view—a real trick in a concrete box with no furniture. Of course, they wanted to know my story right away, and a couple of guys briefed them. I thought having a reputation as a fighter might dampen their curiosity. I was walking a tightrope—stare them down and they might challenge me; shrink from them like the scared young American that I was and they'd pounce like hyenas. I set my jaw and answered their questions in a friendly, no-nonsense kind of way, trying to project the image of a wildcat with good manners. They bought it until they ran out of cigarettes.

About half the guys had tobacco, and there was bartering and favors promised for cigarettes. I was glad it wasn't an issue for me because there were the inevitable arguments as supplies ran low. After the two hard cases had bummed most of the tobacco in the cell, they turned to me. One asked me if I had American cigarettes. I told him I was sorry but I didn't smoke. He said he'd met lots of Americans and they all smoked. I tried to make light of it and told him now he'd met *two* kinds of Americans, hardy har. He and his partner exchanged a few words in Arabic and got to their feet, obviously preparing to approach me. One said the equivalent of "You sure you're not hiding cigarettes from us?" and my mind sprinted into emergency mode, trying to figure out the smart thing to do. If I caved in and let them manhandle me without a protest, I would be seen as weak in a place where weakness could get you killed. On the other hand, fighting in jail wouldn't look good on my Report Card. Plus, I didn't know how many of the twenty-four other Moroccans might decide to show solidarity with their countrymen. I might be able to bust up these two bozos, but I didn't know who might help them. Time was up. They were on me.

I laughed, pulled my sweater over my head and shook it. "How many cigarettes you see in here?" I said in French. I pulled up my pants legs and showed there was nothing in my socks or shoes. I unbuttoned my shirt, pulled my shirt-tail out and flapped it in the breeze. "Whoa! No cigarettes here!" I unbuckled my belt, and I saw some of the other prisoners start to grin. I turned my pockets inside out, then dropped my jeans halfway to my knees and wiggled my butt in my tighty-whitey underwear, getting some laughs and hoots. Even the hard cases were grinning.

Finished with my performance, I held out my arms and said, "Sorry. No cigarettes today." The hard cases shrugged and sat down, and the vise around my gut relaxed. My relief didn't last. True terror was just around the corner.

Chapter Nine:

From Bad to Cursed

I never knew if the guards had come to investigate the noise or if they had another agenda,
but two of them suddenly appeared in the doorway.
I grinned with embarrassment as I buckled my
belt and stuffed my shirt-tail back into my jeans.
Several of the men spoke up about my performance—I could hear 'cigarette' and 'American' in
the babble—and then a general uproar swelled as
the men started crowding the guards asking questions, no doubt the same ones caged men have been
asking for centuries: "Has anybody come to ask
about me? How about some cigarettes? How long
before I go to court? Can my wife bring me some
decent food? If Oman comes and says I didn't do
it, will you let me go?" The guards shouted a few
words but mostly waved their questions away as if
to say "Hey, we're guards, we don't bang the gavel,
put a sock in it." Suddenly I was aware that they
were talking about me, and that the other prisoners
were looking at me in a strange way. Pity? Wonder?
Empathy? What?

"*Qu'est-ce que cé?*" I asked. What's up?

"You don't know when to stop beating a man,"
one of the guards said, the shadow of a wry little

smile on his lips. I swallowed, and my mouth felt full of chalk.

"I know. I went crazy. Is he all right? How badly is he hurt?"

"*Je regrette, monsieur, mais Il est mort.*"

The other prisoners gasped and whispered.

"*Il est mort.*"

I had heard it, but I tried to un-hear it.

"*Il est mort.*"

I couldn't breathe. That's. Just. Not. Possible.

"*Il est mort.*"

He is dead.

I grunted as if I'd been elbowed in the gut.

"No," I said. "You must be mistaken. I didn't kill him, I just—"

The guard glared at me, bared his teeth, spat out a few words and left. My spooning buddy translated for me a few minutes later. The guard had said that Ratface had strangled on his own blood and died. The other prisoners looked at me like I was a condemned man—the friendly ones with pity, the hard cases with little grins as if to say, "Ohh, poor little American. See how much your big rich Cadillac-Big Mac country can help you now."

I felt as weightless as a styrofoam cup, as if all the strength in my muscles and mind had drained out through holes in my feet and left a thin and brittle shell. I knew the hard cases watched to see if I'd cry, so I couldn't. If I saw in my mind's eye an image of my mother or father or brothers, I quickly deleted the image and concentrated on the shape of a hole in the concrete, the arrangement of scabs on my hands, the patterns in the dirt on my shoes— anything to keep my emotions in check.

When the shock thawed, I remembered that Moroccans had often played mind games with me because it gave them a sense of power over a "rich" American who had more than they'd ever have. They might be illiterate and dime-less, but if they knew something I didn't they'd often use it to confuse or disorient me. I once asked a man on a bus if the next stop was the one nearest the square. He assured me it was, and when I got off I saw him and two other men looking at me and laughing because they knew I'd have to walk three miles to downtown Rabat. *Mr. Rich American might have Levis and a pack full of money, but he doesn't know when to get off the bus, hardy har.*

I knew the guards could be doing the same thing. They might be cat-and-mousing me simply because they might never have another opportunity to terrorize an American.

Clinging to that hope gave me a reason to keep breathing; but I spent that night under a crushing, choking dust pile of despair, aware that I might never see anything outside a Moroccan prison.

Late that night, after the snoring had begun, I was still wide awake. My spooning buddy had paired up with someone else, apparently afraid my bad luck would rub off on him. I was actually relieved because I wanted to stay awake and sort my thoughts, make some logical decisions in an illogical situation, come up with a plan for getting through the next hour, the next day, the next—what? The future was a black tunnel in a fog bank.

I did know we were going to be moved to a larger facility soon. I'd heard the others whispering about it, and their fear of The Big House was apparent. Details about the place were sketchy, of course, so we built a grim House of Horrors in our imaginations.

As the others slept, I sat there wrestling for control of my own brain. I knew instinctively that I had to control my fear and try to think rationally; but uncertainty sat on my shoulder like a heavy, ugly, slobbering beast. Ignoring it was like trying to forget a warthog sitting on your shoulders. Just

I devised my plan and rehearsed it a hundred times.

as I would string one reasonable thought to another—"keep a low profile, learn as many Arabic words as possible, don't show your fear"—the beast would tap me with a dirty hoof and scatter my thoughts like fiddlesticks. It would remind me of what I didn't know: If the guards were lying, if Ratface was alive, what I would actually be charged with, how long I would be there, how I would be treated, would I be allowed to communicate with my family or a U.S. official, could I expect to be beaten or even raped in the prison.

Obviously, in such a situation your mind doesn't work the way it usually does. Every decision you make is suddenly weighted with great importance. When another prisoner speaks to you, for example, you have to try to get past the language barrier and quickly interpret the various voice and body clues he's giving you to decide in an instant on the proper response—meaning the response that's most likely to assure your status and safety in the hours and days ahead. You have to decide whether to look into his face with a friendly or neutral expression, or to pretend that you're too busy counting the cracks in the ceiling to pay him much mind, or to clench your jaws and stare a laser beam through his pupils to convey the unambiguous message that you have no fear of him and in fact would rather enjoy the excitement of pulling his tongue out with your bare hands. I used all of those responses and variations on them when I was behind bars, and I was aware of making conscious decisions about ninety percent of the time. It was tiring but necessary.

Back to The Plan. How to proceed? What was I planning for anyway? What could I control? I decided to micro-manage, as I had no real control over whether Ratface was alive or dead, or if I was going to be in a cage in Morocco for a week or a year or the rest of my life. I had to take care of my *immediate* needs, which included not getting raped or strangled by a couple of nicotine addicts or anti-American thugs. And of course Ratface's batty third cousin might slither into my life at any moment looking for vengeance.

The cigarette incident had already demonstrated there was potential for violence, and we were still in the Mayberry of Moroccan lock-ups. If forced to fight someone, I couldn't think of a single positive outcome. If they beat me up (which was entirely possible, by the way—black belts aren't invincible by any stretch), then everybody would know I could be whipped and might take their shot. If I beat them—and when you're fighting more than one you have to attack savagely—I'd make a *minimum* of two permanent enemies and immediately go to the top of the *Doesn't Play Well With Others* list. If I hurt someone as badly as I hurt Ratface, I might get thrown into a dungeon and forgotten. So far, committing mayhem in Morocco had not had a particularly sunny outcome in my life; and I knew that committing violence in a Moroccan *jail* definitely wouldn't get me on the Honor Roll.

With all these things ping-ponging through my mind, I lay there on that icy concrete floor and identified my immediate goal:

Avoid violence by earning respect.

Okay, now I knew what I was planning for. How does one go about this? I remembered reading books about people thrust into survival situations and how they first took inventory of what they had, which seemed logical. There were plenty of things I didn't have—lawyers, guns and money, etc.—but I knew that dwelling on that could only clog my brain and decided not to think about it.

So what was in my Asset column? I had a slightly rattled but generally sound mind. I had my

To reach my ultimate goal, I first had to achieve a much more immediate and specific one.

strength and my health, my clothes, and I spoke French well enough to communicate on a basic level. Was that it? Didn't seem like much. I kept digging. I could sing pretty well. Hmm. I couldn't quite picture myself soothing the savage beasts with "Jambalya and crawfish pie and a filé gumbo. . . ." I had a sense of humor, but even if I had been in the mood, there were quite a few "common reference" obstacles to overcome: "You know when you walk into a 7-11 and—oh, that's right, you don't. Um, well, you know when you walk into a mosque and—"

I had four years of training in *tae kwon do,* but that's what landed me here. And *announcing* it would be viewed either as the desperate crowing of a terrified Westerner, or worse, a challenge to the tough customers who wanted to put a major notch on their *djellaba.* Besides, if I had to use it, I wanted my opponent to be unpleasantly surprised.

Still, it seemed too powerful an asset not to put to use *somehow.* I thought about possibilities, about casually mentioning it, about making a trained but non-aggressive karate move to trigger curiosity and perhaps a question. I leaned against the cold wall at probably 2 a.m., trying to find a comfortable position for my frozen butt while trying to picture possible scenarios when—what the!—I saw a sleeping man's knee move under his *djellaba* in an odd way. Was it a cramp? A dream twitch? His feet remained immobile as his knee writhed bizarrely. Suddenly his knee moved up his thigh and down again! I was transfixed, like I was witnessing a religious vision. After a moment the man jerked and rearranged his legs, and a big rat bolted from under his *djellaba,* raced across an open space, its hairless tail in the air, and disappeared into another cluster of men and *djellabas.* Well, I *never!* Just when you thought you were staying in a Four-Star Lock-up . . . *mammals!* The management will hear about *this,* and they'll be simply *horrified,* of course. Not to mention Ahjmed the next morning, after I told him he'd been violated by a rat the size of a possum. "Oh, yeah, nibbled on your nose-hairs for a little while, didn't you feel the tickle?" Because that's what people do, you see, if they see something you don't. They exaggerate the facts, and—*bam*. It hit me. I figured it out. The winning karate scenario played itself out in my head in the wee hours of the morning. I lay there and worked out the details, and finally decided it was a dicey but reasonable strategy for achieving my goal. At least I had decided on *doing* something. I even fell asleep for a couple of nods.

Chapter Ten:

Clark Kent Hits the Phone Booth

Again, for some reason I never figured out, everyone decided it was daylight and time to stir. Light bulb, concrete, cold air—it looked and felt exactly like it did four-five-six hours ago. But we all groggily reached a consensus and got vaguely vertical. On this particular morning, I had a mission and timing was important. I waited until all but a couple of real dead-heads were awake and stretching, scratching, standing, rubbing their eyes, mumbling and slowly migrating to the restroom.

Adjacent to the cell, through a doorway with no door, was the restroom—spacious at about six feet wide and fifteen feet long—but not very restful. Although I didn't exactly travel first class in Morocco (a laughable understatement, since I never paid more than three bucks for accommodations), I never saw an actual sit-down toilet or toilet paper in the country. Most *toilets* were squat-and-plops: a ceramic depression in the floor with a hole toward the back and two little raised footpads on either side to keep your feet dry. You squatted over the hole, did your business, and used the water to clean yourself and then your hand—which sounds awful to Westerners, but I actually found it oddly difficult to go back to *wiping* after I had been *washing* for awhile. Not to get too graphic, I must confess I now know why *bidets* are so popular in France. It's *refreshing*.

I wondered why every water can was to the left of the toilet until someone explained to me that it was considered *gauche*—and unsanitary—to eat with your left hand. Clean with your left, eat with your right. So much to learn.

Anyway, our restroom didn't have any fancy ceramic depressions. There were just three holes in the concrete floor with water dripping into tin cans beside each one. For obvious reasons, nobody wanted to read *The Marrakech Times* in there, so there was never any pushing or yelling about somebody taking too long. Besides, if you had an emergency, there was always at least one open hole.

I describe this hideous little cubicle in such detail to set the stage for how I put my plan into action. I watched the traffic closely. When the restroom was empty, I hurried inside and went to the far end, where I quickly stretched and warmed up my muscles so I wouldn't injure myself. When I was ready, I positioned myself so I could see the door with my peripheral vision. Before long, I *sensed* someone coming through the door, which was my cue. Keeping my back to the door and carefully avoiding looking at the man, I launched into a *kata*, or series of karate moves which simulates combat with multiple opponents. I kicked imaginary faces, slashed groins, gouged eyes, jumped, spun and chopped these ghost-fighters into quivering piles of bloody mush in about twenty seconds of well-trained fury. I stopped, took a breath, and casually looked at the door, where *two* men stood in shock and awe, their eyes wide and their mouths agape.

"Pardón moi, monsieurs," I said coolly, and walked into the dark hallway. They gave me plenty of room when I stepped between them, and their excited whispers were evidence that my little show

When the time was right to put my plan into action, I didn't hold back.

had had the desired effect. I hoped that, as news reporters, they were as unreliable as they looked. I needn't have worried. They were marvelously unprofessional.

I was still in the hallway, slowly stretching and loosening my muscles, when they came back through and went back to the cell. I avoided looking at them and waited. As soon as they got back to the cell, I could hear them excitedly recounting the astonishing scene they had just witnessed. I stayed in the shadows of the hallway and found a spot where I could see some of the men in the room. It was clear from their reactions and the tone of the storytellers that this *Newsbreak* was being reported vividly and with not a little exaggeration. Later, one of the men in the room told me some of the things my new public relations team reported: I could fly, I could put my fists through brick walls, I could jump as high as a man's head and kick his eyeballs out, I could pull a man's throat out quicker than a snake could strike.

So far, so good.

After a suitably mysterious absence, I strolled back into the room and the whispering abruptly stopped. I glanced casually around the room and immediately sensed my new status as Alpha Male. The few who made eye contact with me all wanted to be my new best friend. The two who had tried to wring cigarettes from me looked a little nauseous. Later, one of them miraculously found an extra blanket he hadn't noticed before and asked if I'd do him the honor of warming myself with it. I thanked him with a benevolent smile, and he reacted as if his death sentence had been commuted. I was Mr. Congeniality after that, which was also part of The Plan: When we were moved into another population of prisoners, I wanted to have the reputation of being friendly, generous, and insanely dangerous. For the first time since I arrived, I actually took a relaxed breath. The very next morning, however, a new storm moved in and sucked that breath away.

Chapter Eleven:

The Big House—Maximum Insecurity

After a sumptuous breakfast of three-day-old bread and water—which was *sooo* much nicer than that dinner of four-day-old bread and water the night before—the guards came in and started barking at us. I practiced my Synchronized Obedience, lining up when everybody else did, moving forward when they did, stopping when a guard pointed at me and concentrating on his gestures, looking for the next clue. Chains rattled, and that primal scrape and clink put an icicle in my throat—slave ships, dungeons, chain gangs.

Two guards we hadn't seen before came in carrying nightsticks and looking very capable of operating them. One made a speech, the meaning of which was clear even to one who didn't speak the language: "We're going to be moving you, and if you don't do exactly what we say immediately, we're going to whack you with these sticks until you get with the program."

They lined up about eight men in the hallway and made the rest of us sit down in the cell. We heard chains rattling, locks locking, men shuffling, guards barking. I was in the next group. About eight of us lined up single file, and a guard handcuffed our right wrists to a single chain. Another guard then clamped leg-irons on the first man in our group and on the last—me. I've never felt less human. I felt more like livestock, a thing on a chain. We began shuffling out and in a moment we saw the light of day for the first time in several days. It was a bright, cool day, but with no joy in the blueness of the sky.

We shuffled to a large truck whose tailgate was down and saw the last couple of guys in the first group still struggling to climb on. For the next few minutes, we tried our best to get onto the truck in a quick and orderly fashion, but climbing while being handcuffed to a group of eight men isn't something you get to *practice*. You get one shot, and it's not easy. A box to use as a step would have helped, but it would have diminished the guards' enjoyment of the spectacle. We helped each other and the guys behind us as well as we could, and we nearly got everybody on board without incident. Then one guy had all his weight on his cuffed hand when his group suddenly surged forward, jerking his hand out from under him and causing his face to slam into the bed of the truck. One of the guards saw it happen and started barking, and I sensed everybody tensing up, afraid the guards might single out somebody to punish. But the face-banger was tough. Even though he was bleeding he was obviously telling them he was okay, his injury was nothing. Later I realized it was fortunate that the guard had seen what happened or we might have to endure an inquisition to see who cracked him in the face.

When everybody was on the truck we rumbled off, then bumped along for about an hour toward the maw of The Unknown. Although we hadn't seen the sky or anything else for several days, nobody was in a tourist mood. Plus, we knew that anybody seeing the truck would gawk, so we kept our heads down out of shame.

Sometimes it was a challenge maintaining a positive attitude.

After awhile the truck slowed and a wave of anxious excitement rippled over us. I stood to take a look and the sight hit me like a brick in the face. We had arrived at *Le Prison Nacionale de Maroc*, which was painted over the massive doors. The National Prison of Morocco. Oh, joy, I thought. Wouldn't my parents be proud.

Guards yelled, papers were shuffled, we were counted and barked at, the tailgate came down and we toddled off, trying to de-truck without slamming our faces into the planks. We'd had a little practice, so skin loss was minimum. Even my cap was still on my head, which thrilled me. I had worn the faded blue French fisherman's cap for more than a year. Not only did it give me warmth, but its familiar feel was like a head-hug from a friend—I didn't feel quite so alone with it hunkered snugly on my scalp. I tugged it down tight before I climbed off because I had a feeling the guards wouldn't be flexible about anybody going back for dropped haberdashery.

The next couple of hours we stood in lines in the sun in a dusty courtyard while guards came and went with papers. I was standing in line when a squatty little guard with a big black mustache stopped beside me and said something to me that sounded like, "Guhalla muk." I said as politely as I knew how in French, "I'm sorry, sir, but I don't understand." He then looked a little peeved and repeated, "Guhalla *muk*," which I didn't understand any better, so he yelled, "GUHALLA *MUK!*" because, as we all know, screaming a foreign language makes it easier to understand since it pierces the brain like an awl. As he yelled it, he grabbed my cap off my head and slammed it into my stomach, doubling me over and knocking the breath out of me. Ah. You wanted me to *guhalla* off my *muk*. Why didn't you *say* so? The learning curve was going to be steep and bruising around here.

Awhile later, an older guard with a white mustache ambled over to me and said, "Deutsch?" and I whisked my cap off so quickly it made him blink. I was hoping my not being German wouldn't disappoint him, but they had my passport so I couldn't lie. "*Non, monsieur, je suis Americain,*" and he reacted as if he was a Yankee fan from way back.

"Ahhh!" he grinned. "Americain! Chee-cah-go?"

I thought, What the hell, and smiled. "Oui, Chicago!" and his huge grin crimped his mustache into a V. He repeated the word several times, grinning all the while. Then he reached in his back pocket and pulled out a rolled-up magazine and handed it to me. It was an English-language *Time* magazine no more than a month or two old. I couldn't believe it. I took it with a grin and a bow and a scrape and two or three *mercis*, and he waved me off as if to say, "Oh, stop groveling, I can't read it anyway." As he walked away, he looked at a younger guard, jerked his thumb back at me and said, "Chee-cah-go!" and the younger guard conceded the older man's worldliness with a grin and a nod.

A *Time* magazine! My God. It was like having a tiny piece of America in my hand, like a warm Big Mac or a baseball or a cold Budweiser. The cover was a cartoon of a gas guzzler weeping from its headlights, with a headline about the American affair with big cars being over. The first big Arab oil embargo was sending gas prices into the stratosphere, which at that time was over fifty cents a gallon. After a quick glance at the cover I rolled it up and put it into my back pocket. I didn't want to see one single word while I was standing out in the sunlight with things to look at. A sparrow might flutter past, a cloud might get in on the act, the fronds of a palm peeking over the prison wall might catch the light in a pleasant way. I sought out things I usually took for granted, feasting my eyes in anticipation of a fast. I can't say that I was ever bored in prison, because I don't think one can be bored and terrified simultaneously. But for a week I had lived with the constant ache of fear in my stomach, joined by the other dull pain of being forced to watch every second of every minute of every hour of every day trudge slowly by with bone-numbing sameness into the past.

No, I would save the magazine until I was in the midst of one of those stultifying periods of nothingness, when the appearance of a fly or a rat was like *"Live! From New York!"*, when the concrete walls slowly closed in as if I were in the bottom of a trash bin. I was going to savor every outdated Watergate story, every photo, every drawing, every ad for Connecticut real estate and package tour to the Bahamas. I wouldn't spoil the delicious surprises each page held until I craved the distraction and needed to visit my little piece of America.

Finally we were herded to our new residence. Our nervous little band of larval inmates shambled into a room the size of a basketball court where about seventy men sat against the walls or lay in clumps and studied us as we filed in. I was looking for a neutral spot to settle when a young bull-necked thug walked up to me and grabbed my magazine. I of course resisted, and he growled, shoved me with his other hand and ripped the magazine from my hand. I felt ninety pairs of eyes watching me to see what I would do. I calmly watched the thug swagger away, then went and found a spot against the wall.

As I suspected they might, my newly-expanded P.R. team immediately went to work. I heard the words *"karate"* and *"Americain"* sprinkled within the inscrutable torrent of Arabic. Heads turned to take a look at me. Within forty seconds, I saw my magazine being passed man to man across the crowded floor in my direction. There had apparently been a misunderstanding. I nodded my thanks to the man who handed me the magazine and he grinned a brown-toothed grin—the first applicant for Best Friend in my new home. Miraculously, the thug who had grabbed my magazine managed to evaporate like a ninja termite. I never saw him again.

After that bit of drama had played out, the men we had joined began to yak with the new arrivals. They craved news from outside, perhaps from relatives or mutual friends, or simply to talk to someone they hadn't seen every day for a month. I noticed a man with a kind expression watching me. I caught his eye and nodded a greeting. He smiled and—loudly enough for a dozen men near us to hear—said in French, "So you are an American?"

"I am," I said with a smile. "I hope that's not a bad thing to be in here."

He smiled. "No, not at all. Americans are...interesting people. May I ask your name?"

I liked this man. He was the first man I would describe as "sophisticated" that I had come in contact with in a week. Unlike most of the dull-eyed potato-heads with whom I had shared concrete, he would have fit right in at a social in Biloxi. I told him my name, though I knew Moroccans had a hard time with the short 'a' in Mack. His name was Abdelatif, which sounded musical compared to my little duck-quack of a name.

"So Meck," he said with a wry smile, "you are an athlete?"

"I try to stay in shape," I said. "And you?"

"No, no. I play a little football, but I'm not a professional."

"Neither am I."

"That's not what I have heard," he said. Several of the men—many of whom were eavesdropping intently—chuckled appreciatively.

"Oh, perhaps my friends exaggerate a bit," I said, hoping the remark would be taken as false modesty.

"Perhaps," he said. "But many of them have seen you do frightening things."

"Really?" I said, genuinely surprised. "How many of them, would you say?"

He was perplexed by the question, then shrugged and said, "A dozen?"

I couldn't help myself: I laughed out loud, which perplexed him anew.

"Why is this amusing?" he asked.

I shook my head and smiled. "This is a fascinating country. There are many interesting people here as well."

We chatted a little longer about where I was from, how I found my way to Morocco, the accommodations at the city jail. After awhile he excused himself, saying he had to prepare dinner. I assumed he worked in the prison kitchen. An hour later, I wished he had.

Chapter Twelve:

Prison 101—Freshman Follies

Around sunset, Abdelatif and a couple dozen
other men started preparing dinner in their corner
of the room. They pulled out baskets of kitchen
supplies they kept neatly stacked with their bedrolls
and lit charcoal on little grills and hibachis. The
aroma of sizzling meats and vegetables soon filled
the room, making the other sixty or seventy of us
salivate. While the lucky ones with families on the
outside dined on freshly-grilled delights, we huddled
masses drank tepid "soup" that had roughly the
same nutritional value as the average American
sink full of dirty dishwater. Perhaps less, actually,
since we Americans leave so much good food on our
plates. I'm sure my children wish I'd never learned
what it felt like to hope for a slice of carrot in a bowl
of gruel, because they think I'm fanatical about not
wasting food. I must admit that after feeling the very
un-American sensation of hunger, the waste in our
country embarrasses me. I think charity begins with
eating all the food you buy and prepare, and that
means eating leftovers until they're gone—much to
my kids' mortification. I know what looking forward
to a three-day-old piece of bread feels like, and it

changed my world view. Sorry, but I don't care how much you give to UNICEF, you're not a good world citizen if every day you throw away enough food for a child to live on.

There is no waste in Morocco, except perhaps near the major cities. Dumps don't exist because there's nothing to dump. If an average American garbage truck were to spill its contents on the street in Fez, within half an hour the citizens would cart off everything but the smell. Trash is burned for heat or plowed into the soil. Food that's not fit for human consumption is either fed to animals or the soil. Or prisoners. So it just makes fiscal sense for the government to allow families to bring food and other necessities to their imprisoned men. Outside the prison, there were long lines of women carrying baskets of edibles and potables to their loved ones every day. Refrigeration was virtually non-existent, so the supply line was constant. Every bite of bread a man's family provided was one less mouthful the king had to buy.

Late that night somebody shouted something and everybody stood up and formed a couple of lines. "Great," I thought. "The first time I've been relatively warm in four days and they're going to move us out to the tundra." Then I saw that we were lining up for blankets, and I felt the same thrill I felt when I was ten and first saw my new bike. They were like army blankets—small and thin—but there was one for every man. I laid mine out and admired it for a moment, arranging it one way, then another. It might have been threadbare, but it was absolutely decadent compared to concrete. I've been under down comforters that didn't give me as much pleasure. It felt downright indulgent. I slept like I was in a Motel 6 at a truck stop.

*   *   *

I was hoping breakfast in prison would be a step up from the three-day-old bread and cold water we got in the jail. It was. They gave us three-day-old bread and prison "tea." Best I could tell, the "tea" was made by dipping a single tea-bag in a five-gallon bucket of water and pulling it out before it got completely wet. The pick-me-up it afforded didn't pick me up very far. You could read the classifieds through a gallon of it. At least it was warm if you were one of the first twenty-five guys in line to the bucket.

After "breakfast" we were instructed exactly how to fold our blankets and handed them over to the guys who stacked them on shelves. We then filed outside to the prison yard, where everybody who wasn't being punished spent most of the day. I would guess there were between 100 and 150 men on the yard at any given time, a good percentage of them sane. The yard was about seventy yards long and forty yards wide and enclosed by a sheer brick wall about fifteen feet high. Our windowless cell was among the dozens behind that wall. Except for two entry doors, there were no architectural features of any kind—no windows, no slits—just sheer brick wall. In the middle of the packed-dirt yard was the laundry and bath area, which consisted of two faucets sticking up from a bricked-over square on the ground, a couple of wooden benches, and two wooden washtubs. A few men bathed and washed clothes, but since the temperature only got up to around 55 during the day, there wasn't a crush of bathers. I suspected the dynamic changed dramatically during the summer and hoped I wouldn't see it. But that needle-point of dread reminded me that there was a very real possibility that I would see many summers there. I put it out of my mind. No sense in worrying until there was something definite to worry about. Micro-manage the moment, I kept telling myself. Move my mind into the next phase of coping when it becomes necessary.

I was walking the perimeter of the yard when I suddenly did a double-take: I thought I saw a blonde man in Levis. Was I hallucinating, or could it be that I wasn't the only non-Moroccan in this place? I approached him immediately and said *hello*.

He was a smiling, gregarious Dutchman named Karel. We quickly exchanged stories. He and his business partner had been arrested for smuggling a car into the country. "We're going home in three days," he said, all smiles. I told him I was very happy for him, but I was sorry that I would be saying goodbye to the only English-speaking person in prison. "Oh, don't worry," he said. "They come and go all the time. You will be moved to the European cell tomorrow or the next day."

The *European* cell? I had no idea. Karel pointed across the yard to a couple of guys I hadn't noticed. They were obviously Westerners, which sent a blip of optimism through my heart. "That's wonderful that you're going home," I said. I asked him how long he'd been in the prison, assuming that it had been a couple of weeks.

"Thirty-two months," he said with a grin. "It goes quickly once you get used to it." He nodded a cheery goodbye and walked away.

Th-thirty-t-two *months* in this hell-hole? For smuggling a car? A victimless crime? I couldn't believe it. I didn't *want* to get used to it.

"Hey, you an American?"

My mind was cloudy, but I turned to see a bearded Anglo about my age. I held out my hand and he took it.

"Yeah. My name's Mack."

"I'm Randy. Your first day?" I nodded. "Yeah," he said, "it's rough at first, but you'll be okay."

"That Dutchman was here for nearly three years for smuggling a car," I said. "I don't think I could handle that."

He chuckled. "A *car*, huh? Try two hundred

cars. Karel and Rutgert were big-time operators. They knew the risk."

I asked him what he was in for. He shrugged. "They caught me with a lousy half a pound. How much did you have?"

Every "European" in the prison except for me and the car smugglers had been caught with hashish, which was illegal to possess outside of a couple of designated growing areas, the most famous of which was Ketama, in the Rif Mountains near the Algerian border. The law was a joke, since you could buy a chunk of hash the size of a Twinkie on any street corner in Morocco, and men lit up in the teahouses everywhere I went. There was even hash in prison. But the authorities would definitely arrest Westerners who possessed a significant amount of hashish, and—based on the anecdotal information I gleaned in prison and in my travels across the country—I'm pretty sure I know why: 1) If Western travelers sell hash to *each other* and take the money out of the country, it does *nothing* for the struggling local economy. And 2) Every "European" I spoke to who had gotten caught with hashish had been betrayed by the very people who sold it to them. Why? It's a great business model: Ahjmed sells a two-pound brick to Steve and advises him that the best place to hide it is in the spare tire of his van. Steve gets to the border of the province, and Muhammed—one of two armed guards in uniform at the checkpoint—immediately goes to the spare tire, opens it up and, surprise, surprise, finds a two-pound brick of hashish and sends a terrified Steve off to prison. Ahjmed gives Muhammed his cut of the profit from the sale, gets his two-pound brick back, sells it to Bob from Cleveland, who just showed up in his van, and tells him the best place to hide it is in the spare tire of his van.

After a month in a Moroccan prison, Steve doesn't care *what* happens to his van and everything in it. As soon as he's released, he hops a train, takes the ferry to Spain, gets on the first flight back to Phoenix, and when he's sitting in his jacuzzi sipping on a Budweiser gives thanks to God for his narrow escape. He doesn't care that Muhammed's brother-in-law has just made a killing selling a nice Volkswagen van to Michel, a Frenchman who can't believe his luck at finding such a fine vehicle at such a terrific price. He needs it to get the antiques he just bought in Meknès back to the ferry in Casablanca, where the van is confiscated by the authorities because the title isn't legal. Michel is happy to escape with his antiques, Muhammed's brother-in-law gets the van back after paying the port official a service charge, and capitalism in a hereditary monarchy marches on, thanks to shaky Western investments.

"I beat up a guy," I tell Randy, who arches his eyebrows. He hasn't met anybody who was in for violence, only aspiring hash smugglers. He shrugs and wishes me luck. I ask him how long he's in for. He says he's leaving the next day after being in prison only two weeks, and he only had to pay one guy a hundred bucks. I try to be happy for him.

Chapter Thirteen:

Mattress Man and Monkeys

I spent one more night in the Big Room and was excited about being transferred to the "European" cell. I thought there might be Italian furniture, maybe a bathtub. Not quite—another concrete box crammed with fifteen roommates, most of them Anglos if not actually European.

There were three white Kenyans who had just been sentenced to six months after authorities found almost forty pounds of hashish welded into a compartment in the wheel well of their van ("It was a scam—the guards went straight to it"). Their claim was that it was "for their personal use." There were two Germans, a Dane, and four Frenchmen, all in on similar charges. Three of the Frenchmen were about my age, but the fourth was a terrified kid with ice blue eyes, black hair, and not a hint of a beard who looked to be about fifteen. His name was Christophe, and he was white-lipped with fear every waking hour. I was only twenty-four, but I knew that this boy didn't belong in prison. He was a child, and reminded me of my sixteen-year-old brother Tim. Seeing him suffer was like watching a baby being slapped. I vowed not to let him be mistreated if I could prevent it.

The only mistreatment would come at the hands of the four or five Moroccans in the cell, a couple of whom were our "hall monitors" and supervised the daily routines of the cell. They were obviously charged with keeping an eye on foreigners and reporting to management. We called them "monkeys" because they were pompous jerks and tended to hoot and howl. Their little power displays sometimes got ugly. They adjudicated our petty disputes, controlled how we lined up for food, when we got our blankets, who got to sleep where, how we lined up to go to the yard, and occasionally even who had to stay in the cell because of some real or imagined infraction. We coexisted in kind of an uneasy truce, because I think they realized that if the ten or eleven of us Westerners decided to kick some Moroccan butt, we could do some severe damage before a guard could break it up. Still, they enjoyed screaming at us when we didn't understand an order, and even pushing and shoving us when they thought they could get away with it—which generally meant when a guard was nearby so we wouldn't retaliate. In short, we hated the arrogant pricks.

I had two run-ins with them, one over a very annoying prisoner in our cell. He was in his sixties, and I suspect he was there for protection from the Moroccan population. He was nuts, and would push and yell if you got too close. With about sixteen men in a room about fifteen feet wide and twenty feet long, uncomfortable proximity was inevitable. When we all lay down on our blankets at night, it was impossible not to touch another man. But what ultimately made him unbearable was his defense of the bedroll he slept on that almost qualified as a mattress. Except at bedtime, all of our blankets were folded and put away, but Mattress Man was allowed to sit on his bedroll next to the wall. Nobody grumbled about it too much at first, in deference to his age—the old guy deserved a little more comfort than us young bucks, even though he was taking up about three times his fair share of square footage. He'd yell and hit you in the legs if you accidentally stepped on the edge of his bedroll, which I suppose was understandable. What finally caused the pot to boil over, however, was his habit of hitting you in the legs if you got *close* to his bedroll, which was *not* understandable or acceptable. One day he hit the Danish guy, who gritted his teeth and mumbled under his breath that he was going to kick Mattress Man the next time he touched him. Three or four of us heard the grumbling and agreed that we were *all* sick of being abused by the guy. A conspiracy was hatched.

An hour later we were doing our usual thing when one of the Kenyans got too close and Mattress Man lashed out, punching him in the leg. "All right, that's it!" the Kenyan yelled, and all ten or eleven of us converged on Mattress Man and started wiping our feet on his precious bedroll. He was, of course, apoplectic, screaming and trying to push us off, but our numbers overwhelmed him. Suddenly, *wham*, I got hit in the shoulder as one of the monkeys waded through the group whacking people and yelling for us to break it up. Nobody fought back—we'd made our point, so we backed away peacefully. Monkey Boy was pumped up with adrenaline, though, and lashed out at whoever was closest. He shoved one of the Germans hard against the wall and kicked another one in the butt. He hit a Frenchman in the chest and I knew I was next in line. Again, a split-second decision, although I was aided by instinct in this one. As soon as he stepped toward me I bared my teeth and snapped into a *tae kwon do* fighting stance. He saved face by gesturing and giving me a look like "I'll deal with you later." Then he turned and shouted a warning to us in French, telling us to leave the old man alone or he'd report us all—which meant we could be locked in the cell for a week or more with no yard privileges.

Our little insurrection worked: Mattress Man was gone the next day, off on his quest to drive every cell in the prison stark raving mad.

*   *   *

There was very little entertainment in the prison. I watched an older man in the yard carving a hash pipe out of a rock, using a slightly harder rock. Sometimes guys would kneel and chant as they prayed, which was a nice diversion. My buddy Abdelatif would chat with me for a few minutes nearly every day. I remember his being pleasantly surprised when I told him that Morocco was the first country to officially recognize the world's newest nation, the U.S.A., in 1776—an arcane fact that I planned to use to butter up a judge if I got half a chance (neither opportunity—to butter up a judge or otherwise use the minutiae to my advantage—ever presented itself). But my favorite entertainment was watching the loudspeaker work. Every day after the midday "meal," the old white-mustachioed guard who had given me the magazine would walk to the center of the yard with a sheaf of papers and use a loudspeaker to make announcements.

He spoke in Arabic, so I couldn't understand much. But every day he'd call out the names of men who were to report to the prison office. In a conversational tone, he'd say, "Mohamed Said Maazouzi." Then his loudspeaker—a strapping young prisoner about twenty years old with a shaved head—would yell, *MOHAMED SAID MAAZOUZI!!* at the top of his lungs. It looked like that *Saturday Night Live* when they made Weekend Update accessible to the hard of hearing: Chevy Chase would say, "In other news tonight," and Garrett Morris would appear in a little circle on the screen, cup his hands around his mouth and yell, *IN OTHER NEWS TONIGHT!!*

It was doubly amusing to me because the

loudspeaker took his job very seriously and never cracked a smile. And also because he wasn't allowed to say anything else, not a syllable, while he was working. I was watching one day when a friend of his walked by and must have said something like, "How long is this going to take?" and the loudspeaker mumbled a quick two-syllable answer and the old guard backhanded him across the chest and gave him a blistering lecture. So he was either dead silent or screaming his fool head off. He'd go from mute as a stone to *AHJMED TASHFIN LEGHZAOUI!!* with no segue—zero to ninety decibels in half a second.

The old man could say those tongue-twisters very fluidly, but completely mangled any non-Moroccan name. *Hans Mogle* might become *Ay-ness Mugololay.* So the Westerners who were hoping to be called would stand close by in a gaggle and listen hard. There was quite a bit of entertainment value in watching them trying to figure out if their name had been called. When the old guy would stumble on a name, chances were good that he was slaughtering a European one and everyone would concentrate intently and watch his lips. He'd say something like, *G-ga-hoon-ata-erz Pk-upom K-ch-ch-halzionj,* and the flustered loudspeaker would sputter, *GAGAHOON-TA POKUPKALZI!!* and the Europeans would look at each other stupefied. Then somebody would slap a German and say, "That was you, Gunter." "Me?!" "Yeah, I heard a *G* I think," and Gunter would run over and ask to see the name.

Like I said, the entertainment choices were limited.

*   *   *

There was some excitement in the yard on the third day. I saw a mob of men and heard shouting, the unmistakable signs of a fistfight. I was as eager to see some action that didn't involve *me* as most guys, so I joined the herd just as guards arrived and the fight was broken up. I craned my neck to see who was involved—a couple of Moroccans, no doubt, since we Westerners shunned the limelight.

I was sickened to see Karel—one of the Dutchmen—stagger out of the crowd, his face a mask of blood. I never got the whole story, but from what I gathered he'd had a run-in with a certain Moroccan bad boy before. The bad boy knew the Dutchmen were going to be released the next day, so he decided to give him something to remember him by. I joined the group of Europeans tending to Karel, who was philosophical even as the blood was being cleaned from several nasty cuts in his face. "I'm okay," he said. "Next week I'll be having a beer and a steak in Amsterdam, and that animal will still be here eating garbage off the floor. Somebody be sure to get that message to him when I'm out of here."

That incident did nothing to diminish the fear I sensed in young Christophe, a thin, pale kid who cringed at gnats. He was simply paralyzed with fear, a good boy trapped in a nightmare with bad men. I couldn't imagine my brother Tim having to survive in that rat cage. I often sat next to Christophe and asked about his family, his hometown, his brothers and sisters, his school, his teachers—anything to get him talking so he could escape the cell (rhymes with *this hell*) for a few minutes as his mind took flight. Sometimes he would even smile for a few moments when he remembered something silly about his family or friends. I considered those moments little victories. I felt that getting him to smile once a day was like giving him a dose of medicine he needed. It got him through to the next day and—for a moment, anyway—helped him see a glimmer of light through the fog of hopelessness.

After the fight, I sought Christophe out just so he wouldn't feel alone and vulnerable. I had only been in the prison for six or seven days, but I had seen the monkeys slap him just to hear him whimper, grab him by the neck and throw him into line. I had heard that they took food from him.

A couple of nights later I found a piece of potato in my soup—a rarity that I took as a good sign. Had the meal ended without incident, I probably wouldn't have remembered it.

When the food was distributed on that particular night, I was on the other side of the cell but noticed a monkey hovering close to Christophe. Like many of us, Christophe crossed his legs and balanced his bread on his knee while he drank his soup. Monkey Man suddenly reached over and snatched the bread off his knee. Christophe instinctively grabbed at it, and Monkey Man hit the boy's shoulder with his fist and hissed at him menacingly. Christophe slumped against the wall and despondently drank his soup. The theft of your evening bread was not insignificant. We were given exactly enough food to keep us healthy and no more. There were no blubber butts in prison. If part of your ration was taken away, you got hungry. If you got hungry too often, you got weak. If you got weak, you got sick. To take basic nutrition away from another prisoner was as serious as beating him.

I exchanged looks with a few guys who'd seen what had happened, but it was clear that none of them was going to raise a hand. When it was a European's word against a Moroccan's, the argument was lost before it began. Still, I couldn't let it go (what can I say?—it's a curse) but I had to play my hand carefully. I couldn't afford to get into a scrape now. I walked over and wedged myself between Christophe and the bread thief, giving my little friend a cheery greeting. Monkey Man knew immediately why I was there and moved the bread out of reach. I noticed his hands were trembling. The conversational hum in the cell faded to near silence because almost everyone knew what was happening and wondered what I was going to do. I handed Christophe my piece of bread, and Monkey Man noticed. In fact, he was keenly aware of my every move. I could tell he didn't want to be the one to find out for sure if I was as dangerous as advertised. I also noticed that he didn't take a bite of his ill-gotten bread, which he had set on a jacket on the floor beside him. We often spread pieces of clothing on the floor to sit or eat on.

I needed to deflect the attention. I called to a German across the room: "Hey Niklas, did you get to meet your lawyer when they called you in today?"

Niklas frowned comically. "No, he was busy with a big case. He's suing somebody for three *dirham.*"

All the English-speakers laughed. Three *dirham* was about seventy-five cents. That started the general chatter again, so Monkey Man and I were no longer the center of attention. Christophe whispered, "I can't take your bread," and tried to hand it back to me. Very quietly, so only Monkey Man and Christophe could hear, I said, "Our friend here is lucky. He has two pieces. Maybe if I'm nice he'll give me one of his." I then gave Monkey Man a cold little smile while staring him directly in the eyes. I hadn't made a big announcement or challenged him in front of the other prisoners. I had given him a way out, and I was impressed with his exit strategy. He didn't even have to hand the bread to me. He simply got up in a huff and stomped away, dramatically showing me his back as if he didn't want to sit next to me because I stunk. I was of course *crushed* that Monkey Man didn't want to dine with us, but I got over it. I took the bread, Christophe nodded his thanks and we ate in silence. I remember hoping that he'd get released before I did, because who would protect him? But the knot didn't untangle that way.

Chapter Fourteen:

Professional Skinny Dipping and Rednecks with Shotguns

Some might wonder how—or even *if*—I can remember such moments as the bread thief incident in such detail after so many years. It's no mystery to me. You've heard people describe how a dramatic event—a car wreck, a robbery, an earthquake—suddenly seemed to unfold in slow motion. What they mean is that every millisecond suddenly became so extraordinary and vivid that the extraneous world ceased to exist and they focused all of their senses on the event they were witnessing. In a movie camera, slow motion is achieved by speeding up the film that's being exposed, so that when it's replayed, it takes several times longer than real time for the captured action to play out. Instead of the batter's homerun swing being a half a second, it's stretched out to three seconds, showing us tiny slices of time that our brains usually don't process. Being imprisoned in a foreign country was by far the most dramatic and intense event in my life to that point. I was hyper-aware of every passing moment, of every image, of every smell and sound. My brain was whirring like a high-speed camera, processing my environment with astounding clarity, in living color and even smell-a-vision. When I chose to re-play some of those moments, sometimes years later, they unspooled from my brain as if the picture had been taken yesterday.

I didn't unspool it for anyone else for quite awhile. As I said before, I had been safely home for years before I could really talk to anyone about it, which no doubt seems strange to those who can't imagine life without a therapist. Some people can't even buy groceries without calling a friend to share every melodramatic moment, from the horrible parking situation to the picked-over tomatoes and snippy cashier. To some, the drama of life simply has to be shared and recounted or it has no meaning, no joy, no heft.

I understand that unburdening oneself can be cathartic—I've done it and it's been very therapeutic in certain situations. It probably would have been beneficial to talk about the prison experience, too. I suppose I should have sought out the right person and the perfect situation and let it all gush out, allowing the tears to flow and my gut to buckle as I re-lived the terror of my darkest moments. It probably would have melted some of the fear that had dried to a crust around my heart. But for years I never had the slightest urge. I didn't feel I was suppressing anything, any more than I was suppressing the urge to drive a nail through my thumb or dive through a plate glass window. I could live very comfortably without dredging up the pain. Until you've been locked in a cage like a zoo animal, with absolutely no certainty that you'll ever be released, you can't really understand the crippling emotions that fester in your consciousness. Until you've been totally at the mercy of men who can literally decide whether you'll live your life like a man or a farm animal, then you probably can't relate to the horrors that inched through my brain like an insidious platoon of worms. Until you've had those worms infesting your thoughts, you probably can't understand why you never, ever want to feel them boring through your psyche again. You don't want them to stir. You want them to stay coiled in their holes, inert, forever. If you're in a social situation, for example, and someone makes a comment that disturbs a worm hibernating deep inside your skull, and you feel the worm pulse and flex, preparing to burrow out of its nest, your reflex is to squash it immediately—you tell a joke, or plunge your hand into ice water for a beer, or clap to the music, or go to the john and splash water in your face and jerk the paper out of the dispenser as you count the sheets aloud, One, Two, Three, Four, Count the Sheets and Kick the Door. You smother that worm and try to put it back to sleep, because you know the little bastard can still put a vise-grip on your intestines and make you cry, and you don't want to have to explain that.

Which is not to say I was morose when I returned to the States. Quite the opposite, in fact. After dealing with it awhile, I trained myself to quickly turn the emotion around. When an unwelcome memory would suddenly flash across my consciousness, I'd immediately shift my focus to wherever I found myself at that moment, and a warm flood of gratitude would wash over me and shoo the worms into hiding. *You could be eating gruel in a dungeon in Africa*, the memory might say, but here you are picking out a succulent peach in a produce market, or cheering for your younger brother at a baseball game, or digging into fries and a burger, or floating down a pristine creek in a canoe and eating a big, sloppy roast beef sandwich. Life was more than good. Life was spectacular. I wanted to grab it and hug it and eat it and make the most of every second.

So, when I got back home to my ecstatic and welcoming parents (who didn't have a clue I was a jailbird, of course), I made the most of mooching off them, hugging relatives and eating life and Mom's cooking. I hoped to pass a pleasant month or so like that as I gradually transitioned back to my native land and normalcy. Then, like an annoying guest who arrives too early, a job possibility came out of nowhere after I had been transitioning and mooching for less than a week.

I was compelled by duty—and my father, who has an exceptionally low tolerance for moochers—to apply for it. I didn't know if I could hug life and punch a clock at the same time; but if any job might make it possible, being a reporter on a brash young newspaper would have to be high on the list. When I went in for the interview, I didn't tell my future employers that my experience included observing the inner workings of a foreign prison; but then, I had no way of knowing at the time that the experience legitimately deserved a place on my résumé. Neither did I know that being a newspaper reporter would put me in a position to have more law enforcement officials yelling at me and aiming guns at me. I soon realized that my ordeal had taught me much more than how to fall asleep on concrete. It taught me how to function coolly and intelligently with fear gripping my throat. It taught me that there are far worse things than having a school board member mad at you, or being thrown out of a meeting for asking a question, or having a CEO scream at you while thirty employees glare needle-holes into you. If I had never shuffled into a Third World prison in leg-irons, those things might have flustered me. If I had never had a soldier yell at me in Arabic while aiming a machine gun at my face, the screaming CEO might have intimidated me. But that CEO scared everybody in that room *but* me, and I made sure he knew it. I had spooned with a thug to stay warm. Stripping down to my notebook to interview a nudist in the Mississippi woods was nothing. My training had taught me that the greatest fear is indeed fear itself.

My editor stood at my desk with a smug look on his face. "Somebody just applied for a business license to open a nudist camp in Hancock County," he said, handing me a slip of paper with driving directions. "Don't forget your camera."

The Baptists were in an uproar, not surprising considering that Hancock was one of the most conservative counties in one of the most conservative states in the known universe. An Air Force officer—a godless Yankee, no doubt—who was stationed at Keesler Air Force base in nearby Biloxi, had been hosting weekend retreats for like-minded naturalists for a couple of years on a remote acre he'd cleared in the middle of the deep piney woods a good five miles from the nearest paved road, State Highway 49. He and his wife and two kids enjoyed the camaraderie and freedom of clothes-optional fun, but it had gotten so popular that he was going to have to start charging admission so he could pay for basic services like water and power. Being a law-abiding citizen, and finding that no local or state law specifically prohibited the establishment of a nudist camp, he applied for a business license. After my story appeared, you'd have thought Satan himself had applied to open a whorehouse and porn studio on the front lawn of the First Baptist Church. Citizens wrote angry letters to the newspaper, hissing about the moral degradation and general brain rot a nudist camp would inevitably visit on the county, and probably the whole state. Preachers howled that God would strike county officials a vicious blow if they allowed this modern-day Gomorrah to take root in the very bosom of Christian family values (interestingly, the Christian families didn't make a peep a few months earlier when I had covered a Ku Klux Klan rally in a field owned by one of them).

On a typically humid June day, I drove four or

five miles down a dirt road until I got to a mud hole that looked like it might swallow my old Plymouth Satellite whole. A light drizzle had begun, so the hole would be even mushier on my return. I pulled off the road and started walking through the light rain, wishing I had remembered to bring an umbrella or a raincoat. In my standard reporter uniform—slacks, cotton shirt and tie with no jacket—I wasn't really equipped for a trek into the wilderness. I walked a quarter mile or so to a shell driveway that was blocked by a padlocked gate. Signs on the gate named the retreat and its proprietors and said No Trespassing. Having learned hard lessons at various border crossings—and wanting to postpone having another gun pointed at me for as long as possible—I started yelling to get someone's attention. Dogs started barking—another good reason not to make any impulsive moves—and after a moment an eight-year-old girl in shorts appeared thirty yards away and asked me what I wanted. I told her I was a newspaper reporter and would like to talk to her mom or dad. She told me to wait, then came back a minute later and yelled that I could come in, but I'd have to wait for her dad to come home from work to talk to anyone. Perfect. Good reporters are like door-to-door salesmen—if they can get in the door, they can usually get what they want.

There was a neat mobile home on one end of the property, which wasn't much larger than the standard yard in that part of the country. There was a swimming pool, a sand volleyball court, several picnic tables and lounge chairs on the well-kept lawn under a few pine trees. There were kid's toys scattered about and a shed with yard tools and a lawnmower. Nothing suggested that I had walked into a nest of iniquity.

The little girl had gone back inside and shut the door, and I heard her mother's voice inside. I knocked on the door, and an attractive thirty-something woman wrapped in a beach towel opened the door. On most assignments, my brain was the only organ that got stimulated. Knowing she was naked under the towel provoked some unprofessional stirrings in an area closer to my knees. Maintaining professional detachment and cold objectivity was going to be a chore, because I'm a guy, and a part of my brain was trying to make that towel fall.

I introduced myself, but instead of asking if I could speak to her a few moments—which she'd have a quick and negative answer for—I told her how wonderful their little oasis was and asked if it had looked like this when they bought it. I knew it hadn't, but if I could get her talking she might at least give me all I'd need for a bare-bones story if her husband chose to throw me off the property instead of talking.

"Oh, God, no," she said, laughing at the memory. "It was just woods and briar patches, but I—"

"Wow, so you really did carve this incredible place out of the wilderness," I said, looking out at the grounds and not at her. "Did you hire it all done or did you and your husband swing an axe, too?"

"David did a lot of work—we all did—but we had to hire a few guys with heavy equipment to do some of it. Listen I—"

"But it looks great, so how long ago was that?"

"We started clearing it in '74, right after we bought it, but—"

"In '74?! Holy smokes, it looks like it's been here for twenty years. Your daughter must love it. She's a real cutie. Do you have other kids?"

"My son Evan is five, but listen I—"

"Wow, I wish we'd lived in a place like this when I was five. Does he—"

"Excuse me, Mr. Dryden, please," in a not-unfriendly way. She actually complimented me on getting her to talk when she said she wouldn't, so I knew I wasn't dealing with a dummy. "I know why you're here," she said, "and I know everybody thinks we're freaks, but I don't want to say any more until my husband gets here around 4:30."

I looked at my watch. "Ouch. That's another two hours, and I've got a deadline," I said. "I really don't have that much to ask, if you'd just tell me if—"

"No, really, I'm not going to talk anymore," she said, closing the door.

"Wait! Okay." I said. "I understand. But I'm not one of the people who thinks you're freaks." And then my training really kicked in: *This is nothing. I've walked in leg irons.* "I've got some time to kill. Can I take a swim?"

She looked at the cool drizzle dripping off the pine trees and gave me a skeptical grin. "Sure."

"Mind if I leave my clothes on the porch so they don't get soaked?"

Another grin, more skeptical than the first.

"Be my guest," she said, and closed the door.

I undressed completely and walked naked through the grass to the pool, praying it was warmer than the rain. It was, so I cannonballed in, making as big and loud a splash as possible. I did a few laps, sneaking peeks at the windows on the trailer. After a few minutes, the curtains parted slightly at a window in the back, and I knew I was being watched. I quickly got out and did a flip off the side of the pool so they'd know that I was thoroughly, undeniably naked. Since I was familiar with their lifestyle, I didn't worry about scarring impressionable youngsters.

Some might say I was foolhardy for stripping down in the presence of another man's wife, but it was a carefully calculated risk. I knew there was a possibility that her husband might come home early and find a naked man on the property with his wife and kids. In most circumstances, that would be awkward at the very least and grounds for a summary execution at worst. You'd be hard pressed to find twelve citizens of Hancock County who'd convict any husband who discovered such a situation and demonstrated his disappointment with a shotgun. But I thought it was reasonable to assume that being a naked man in a nudist camp wouldn't be judged too harshly by a nudist, and that being a naked *reporter* who obviously had no moral axe to grind could earn me some major brownie points. Rarely has a risky assumption paid off so well.

After I'd paddled around in the pool for twenty minutes, the sun came out, which I interpreted as a rather heavy-handed Sign from God that the resident sun-worshipper might be more approachable than when I'd arrived. I got out of the pool, strode to the door of the mobile home and knocked. When the woman opened the door, I stood facing her in Full Monty position and asked if I could borrow a towel. She nodded with a friendly expression—she knew she was looking at one of the few adults in southern Mississippi who didn't judge her or condemn her lifestyle as perverted. I thanked her when she handed me the towel, remarked on what a lovely day it had become, and said I was going to put my pants on and cool off in a lounge chair in the shade of a pine tree. I asked if she'd like to grab a couple of cold drinks and sit and chat with me for a few minutes. She said she guessed that would be all right, and a few minutes later we were sitting in lounge chairs enjoying some southern sweet tea. I told her I had spent a week at a nude campsite on a beach in France, and made her laugh with my description of the nude marching band that *oompah*-ed down the beach on Bastille Day wearing only boots and hats. In no time we were yakking like old friends. I didn't want to scare her off by pulling out my notebook, so I made copious mental notes as we went along.

When her husband drove up, the kids ran to

him and he picked them up and made them giggle. Then his wife greeted him with a kiss and a hug. In his crisp Air Force uniform and surrounded by his loving family, he could never pass as one of Satan's minions. I stayed a good forty yards away under the pine tree to give his wife a chance to fill him in on the events of the last couple of hours. The ice had been thoroughly broken, of course, so he shook my hand with a smile and invited me into the trailer.

The fundamentalists were not happy with my description of this affable, intelligent, loving couple and their cute, well-scrubbed and well-behaved kids. Since I didn't depict a bunch of scaly devil worshippers living in depravity, an uproar naturally ensued. The newspaper became a lightning rod, deluged with letters from both the Outraged Right and the Outgunned Left. As long as we were being hit by only letters and not firebombs, my editors were happy. And since I was the only journalist on the coast who got the story from the source, they were so pleased that they entered the piece in the Louisiana-Mississippi Associated Press Writing Competition. I won First Place for Spot News Reporting that year. I didn't give Ratface any of the credit, but I could have.

The next time my training got me through a tough situation as a reporter, there was quite a bit more at stake: I had yet another gun pointed at me and watched a man die.

*   *   *

Sunday is a slow news day whether you work for the *South Mississippi Sun* or *The New York Times*, which is why it's an off day for most of the news staff. No court cases are argued, no laws are passed, disgruntled postal workers have no one to shoot at. At the *Sun,* we beat reporters took turns coming in on Sunday to handle the shoplifting arrests, traffic accidents, and drunk-and-disorderly calls that trickled in. Until this particular Sunday, the most interesting incident I had reported was when a woman accused a man of assaulting her at a cheap motel. On the affidavit under "Weapon Used," the investigating officer had written "Tongue." But Sundays were usually dull, so we typically spent most of the day writing feature-type "fluff" pieces that weren't time sensitive and checking the stories that came over the AP wire to help the city desk editor cull the juicy from the junk.

One Sunday I was on duty when the police radio on the editor's desk started crackling with unusual activity, and it was soon apparent that a serious situation was developing. A man had gone to a woman's mobile home (not everybody in Southern Mississippi lives in trailers, but it seems that news-makers tend to), and neighbors called the police after hearing terrified screaming and threats of violence. Police arrived and tried to defuse the situation, but the man got more agitated and told the police he'd kill everybody in the house if they didn't leave. After a tense few minutes, the terrified woman emerged from the trailer, an infant clutched to her chest, and the muzzle of a .45-caliber pistol pushed against her cheek. As police looked on helplessly, the man forced her into his car and drove away.

I had my jacket on, my camera loaded, my notebook packed, and my keys in my hand, ready to bolt in an instant. But the situation was still fluid, and my editor didn't want me chasing police cars all over the county. We didn't have to wait long, because the drama unfolded pretty quickly. The man headed north up State Road 57, a welcome development for law enforcement because he was headed away from populated areas, out in to the sticks. Before long, however, he'd cross the county line, which would complicate matters for law enforcement on both the Jackson County side—where the drama began—and in George County, which was considerably more rural and didn't have nearly as much manpower or equipment as their coastal colleagues. In an effort to avoid sticky jurisdictional matters as well, it seemed prudent to keep the incident in Jackson County if at all possible. Sheriff's deputies quickly stopped all traffic both ways on 57 and stretched a spiked strip across the highway about a mile south of the county line.

Soon we heard the report that he had hit the strip and his tires were deflating, but apparently not fast enough to prevent him from making it into George County (to prevent dangerous blowouts that could endanger innocent people, the strips are armed with hollow spikes that embed in the tires and gradually deflate them rather than ripping them apart on impact). We heard the sheriff deploy a team of sharpshooters beside the road, and they shot out what was left of the tires about 300 yards south of the county line. Shuddering and swerving on metal rims, the guy pulled into the parking lot of a country church. My editor said, "Be careful," and I sprinted out to cover the most challenging—and frightening—incident of my career.

When I got to the church, there were about six patrol cars and a mob of officers from various agencies in the parking lot, plus a handful of civilian onlookers. The man had taken his wife and baby into the adjoining cemetery. As she sat on a tombstone, the man stomped around shouting and waving the gun in the air. I hid my notebook, approached a deputy and asked him what the situation was. He pointed to the woods on two sides of the cemetery and said there were three police snipers with their guns trained on the man at all times. They were under orders to shoot to kill if he looked like he was about to shoot his wife or if he fired the pistol in the direction of the police, who were all hiding behind trees, cars, and the church. So the hostage was his wife and the baby was theirs? The deputy said yes and then got suspicious. He asked me if I was a reporter, and I had to admit that I was. He cursed under his breath, clamped his jaw tight and walked away. He could get his badge yanked for talking to the media without permission.

A reporter from a competing newspaper showed up, and I caught her up on what I knew as a professional courtesy and so she wouldn't have to ask the same people the same questions. We knew it would be prudent to keep as low a profile as possible and not become a nuisance in such tense circumstances. After another few minutes, Sonny, a photographer from my newspaper, showed up and I briefed him. He took some photos of the police, then put a huge lens on his camera to get some long-distance shots of the hostage-taker and his victims.

A couple more reporters straggled in, and we were standing in a group when Jackson Country Sheriff John Ledbetter pulled up in his squad car and his deputies briefed him. Then we were uncomfortably aware that he was pointing and they were all looking at us. A moment later, two deputies came to tell us that, for our own safety, we'd have to withdraw from the area. We complained, of course, assuring them that we'd stay behind the church, well out of the way, but they had their orders and—ignoring our arguments—escorted us to a pullout beside the road about a hundred yards north of the church. They issued a very stern warning to us, saying that any reporter caught outside the designated area would be subject to arrest. We asked if someone could at least give us occasional updates, and they assured us that we'd be kept informed. When they were out of earshot, we all agreed that we'd be forgotten as soon as they got back to the churchyard—which turned out to be true.

For the next two hours, we waited beside the

road, chatting, killing time, comparing bosses, etc., and sending a scout back to the churchyard every half hour or so to see if there were any new developments—which there never were. Our impatience and frustration began to grow when various civilians in pickup trucks and cars pulled into the parking lot to see what was going on and started hanging out with the police. After awhile, it looked like a church social, and we were only ones in the county not invited. This was unacceptable. I had a job to do, and it wasn't getting done. I decided to *Control my Fears* and *Take Bold Action,* because this path to my goal wasn't working. I told Sonny I was going to see what I could find out, and he nervously reminded me that I could be arrested. *I've been in a federal prison in Morocco,* I thought. *Spending a night in jail in my hometown would be merely interesting.* I joked that if I got hauled in I'd just do a feature on jail conditions. I took off, leaving the other six or seven news people to discuss whether I was being foolhardy, or if they should defy the deputies' orders, too.

I got to my car and headed south, figuring there might be more law enforcement posted away from the church in case the guy tried to run for it. I might even find a policeman who didn't know that reporters had been banished from the area. I hadn't gone far when I saw a car parked on the shoulder and an older, obviously anxious woman pacing beside it. No one else was around, so I figured I'd see if she knew anything. When I got out, I noticed that she could actually see the cemetery through the trees from her vantage point, and that she'd been crying. She was obviously a distraught relative—I had struck gold. I didn't know how she might feel about reporters, so I decided to be a tad less than completely forthcoming. I didn't lie, but I admit that I let her draw her own conclusions.

"Excuse me, ma'am," I said. "Could you please identify yourself and tell me your connection to this case?" I suppose I looked and sounded a bit like a detective, all business in my shirt and tie and notebook in hand. *Just the facts, ma'am.*

Holding back tears, she told me her full name, and that she was the mother of the woman being held hostage. I asked her if she would please give me the full names of the three people in the cemetery, "because we want to make sure we have all our information correct." She told me, including middle names, and spelled them for me. I asked her what the man did for a living and where he worked, all of their ages, how long the couple had been separated, what exactly had happened at the trailer that morning, if he'd threatened her daughter before, if he'd been drinking, if he had a police record, if the police had asked for her help in negotiating, if her daughter had called the police before, if the man seemed suicidal or unbalanced, who his parents were and where they lived—and she had clear and precise answers for every single question.

By the time I thanked her and told her to be careful, I had all the background information necessary for a complete story *(I've changed all the names to protect family members who might prefer that the incident continue to fade into history)* The other reporters knew "a guy" was holding "a woman" and a child hostage. I knew that Ronald Taylor, 33, a pipe-welder at Ingalls shipyard in Pascagoula, was holding his estranged wife JoAnne, 31, and their six-week-old son Jason. I knew that Taylor had been raised by his grandmother, a Mrs. Elroy, and that JoAnne's mother Irene—my source—had been in the trailer and witnessed the abduction. All I needed to do now was see how it played out and report what happened.

As I started back to the churchyard, I decided to try to increase my chances of infiltrating the pack of onlookers. I got a baseball cap and a t-shirt out of my trunk and took off my shirt and tie. *I've had*

*a Moroccan border guard aim a machine gun at my
heart. This is nothing.*

I put on a green cap and matching t-shirt
emblazoned with G & G BUILDING SUPPLIES, hoping
my softball "uniform" would help me blend into the
growing population of rubberneckers. Police officers
tend to take note of vehicles, so I put my camera
and some extra film into a plastic bag I found in the
ditch and walked along the road back toward the
churchyard. When I got there, Sonny and the other
reporters were still clumped together in the pullout
a hundred yards down the road watching me. I had
a feeling they wouldn't be there much longer.

By that time there were at least twenty police
officers on the scene, making me wonder who was
protecting the rest of the county. The parking lot
was crowded with a couple dozen onlookers leaning
on pickup trucks, squatting in circles, smoking, dipping snuff, talking quietly. About sixty yards away
in the cemetery, I could see Taylor holding the pistol
as his wife JoAnne and an older woman I assumed
was Mrs. Elroy sat on a tombstone with the baby. I
looked around for a safe source and chose a civilian
who seemed to be following the action. He confirmed
that the older woman was Mrs. Elroy, who had been
summoned to try to talk him into giving himself up.
Other than that the story hadn't changed much, so
I wandered around as inconspicuously as possible,
surreptitiously snapping photos of armed police
officers, spotters looking through binoculars, the
sheriff conferring with his troops, clutches of spectators. Even if Sonny were unable to get anything,
with those photos in the can we'd at least have
something to go with the story.

I was lining up another shot when I heard
yelling, and every officer I could see suddenly tensed
and crouched, looking into the cemetery, their weapons at the ready. All conversation within earshot
abruptly stopped. In the anxious silence broken only

by the rustling of leaves and Taylor's unintelligible bellowing, I realized for the first time how tense the situation was, how frayed nerves already were. Taylor waved the pistol as he paced in front of the women, who sat on the gravestone flinching at his blistering tirade. The more his grandmother tried to calm him, the more agitated he became. From my position I could see Sheriff Ledbetter watching the action from behind a squad car, his foot on the back bumper. He was sweating, literally and figuratively. He was the Man In Charge, and several lives depended on decisions he'd have to make. He could have ordered his snipers to kill Taylor hours ago; but he was obviously hoping to avoid violence if at all possible. Taylor suddenly took Mrs. Elroy by the arm and pushed her toward the parking lot. He was yelling, but I couldn't make out many words. When she stumbled away, I could see at least five rifles aimed at Taylor, ready to fire if the sheriff gave the order. Ledbetter watched the man intently, his jaw muscles working. I saw him say something to the deputy beside him and my mouth went dry. A moment later, I saw the snipers relax. He had ordered them to stand down.

After the ripple of excitement had smoothed out and people began to mill and talk again, I struck up conversations with whoever would talk, hoping to pick up whatever tidbits that might help me fill the story out. I spotted a particularly anxious civilian and found out he was Taylor's brother Andrew, who kept saying to anyone who'd listen, "He wouldn't shoot anybody, I know him, he's just mad, he'll cool down." He knew a lot of the cops wanted to blow his demented brother away now, before he hurt a woman or—God forbid—a six-week-old baby. I was watching him once when his brother exploded into a bellowing tirade out in the cemetery, and Andrew's face turned the color of ice. He seemed to kind of weaken and cave in on himself, like he knew Ronald was committing suicide and there was nothing anyone could do to stop him.

Suddenly there was activity and the cops were on high alert again. Taylor was walking his hostages back toward their car in the parking lot. After letting them swelter on a marble gravestone in the blazing sun for a couple of hours, he'd finally agreed to let his wife move the baby into the relative comfort of the car. My guess is he chose it because it was the only place on the property he had any claim to, it might have air conditioning, and it would allow them more privacy than sitting under a tree. And with its tires reduced to jagged ribbons, it was without doubt the only vehicle the sheriff would have allowed him to enter. The choice seemed odd, however, since they were walking about fifty yards back into the thickest concentration of lawmen, who started pulling back and moving everybody along as soon as they saw what was happening. As I moved back, I saw that the other reporters had decided the deputies were too busy to notice them moving to the front. Like me, most of them kept well out of the way on the periphery of the action. That included Sonny, who smiled nervously when I spotted him and gave him a thumbs up. He shrugged, embarrassed. He'd gotten there just before the migration back to the car and had used his huge zoom lens to get some good shots of Taylor and the hostages out in the open.

The only reporter who didn't make himself inconspicuous was a guy we'll call Meatball—an obese, sloppy bigmouth with memorable B.O. who wrote, edited and published a weekly paper in Biloxi and loudly reminded us at every press conference that he deserved equal access to newsmakers, regardless of his comparatively miniscule circulation numbers. "We're as legitimate a voice of the people as any of you big guys," he would spout, so we weren't surprised when he quickly went from asking deputies questions to *demanding* information. I was telling a reporter from Pascagoula that this jerk was going to get us all rounded up and exiled to the pullout again if he didn't shut up when I heard a deputy shout "Sit!" between clenched teeth. Meatball stammered a protest, which made the cop madder. "Sit! Down! There! Now!" he yelled, his nose an inch from Meatball's moist schnoz. With much grunting and awkward realigning of cellulite, Meatball used the trunk of a blackjack oak to lower himself to the ground. He looked around for support, as if to say, "Can you believe this guy?" He got nothing but glares from the rest of us.

For the next hour, the grandmother shuttled between the car and the sheriff, taking messages, water, formula for the baby—whatever the negotiators thought was prudent to let them have. On her second or third trip, she hurried away from the car carrying a balled-up blanket, and the news spread quickly: "She's got the baby! She's got the baby!" and a general sigh of relief went up as weeping relatives gathered the tiny bundle up like a football and quickly took it out of harm's way. It was the first and only good news since the crisis began, and I could sense optimism vibrating through the crowd. But as the shadows got longer, so did the chances for a peaceful ending.

I had found a position that was far enough away from the car—about forty yards behind the left rear fender—so the lawmen wouldn't make me move, yet close enough that I had an unobstructed view. The sun began to set in the woods behind the church, and the deepening gloom settled on the car and the tense assemblage of humanity surrounding it. I could hear snatches of conversation among the lawmen. They were concerned that the darker it got, the less control they would have over the situation, and the less chance they would have of preventing a tragic ending. With every passing moment, their options dwindled dangerously.

Taylor was in the front seat on the passenger side, JoAnne behind the wheel, and Mrs. Elroy used the left rear door to go in and out. After the baby had been rescued, I saw Mrs. Elroy nodding as the sheriff gave her instructions for her next visit to the car. When I later found out what he'd instructed her to do, an ice-ball formed in my gut. She had no way of knowing that she was agreeing to help the lawmen kill her grandson. When she got in the back seat, I watched closely to see if I could tell what she was doing. As they talked, I caught only glimpses of the top of Taylor's head as he slouched low in the seat so the lawmen couldn't see him. Then I saw the left rear window being rolled down very slowly. It would come down an inch, then stop, come down another inch and stop. When it was open about half-way, Mrs. Elroy gradually eased across the back seat to the other side, talking awhile, moving an inch, pretending to adjust so she could see one of them better, until she was on the other side of the car. Then the glass in the right rear window slowly began to drop until there was about a ten-inch opening. I later learned the sheriff had told her to roll the windows down so they'd have a clearer view of what was happening in the car. That was true, but he failed to mention that it would also give his shooters a clearer line of fire.

A television news van from Mobile suddenly pulled into the parking lot. When the three-man crew got out, a couple of deputies went over to warn them of the danger and to keep them back. As the deputies briefed the crew, the cameraman nodded "gotcha" as he shouldered his equipment, the reporter nodded "you bet" as he straightened his tie, the sound man nodded "absolutely" as he tested the microphone, and then they completely ignored what they'd been told and started walking briskly toward the front line, where jumpy officers were focused intently on trying to keep a deranged man from blasting the life out of a terrified young woman. The deputies took a more urgent tone and tried to head off the crew, but, like all self-important television crews whose goal was to provide "tape at eleven," the crew kept chugging forward as if their mission gave them every right to ignore the orders of police officers. Sheriff Ledbetter heard the commotion, spun around, saw what was happening and yelled out for his deputies to stop the goddamned TV people NOW! About six deputies converged and grabbed the three and started shoving them back. Cables got tangled, the camera got jerked, a microphone dropped, there was scuffling and cursing, the reporter barked at the deputies that they had no right to push him around—while several of us looked at each other, shaking our heads and thinking, "Actually, he's got every right to club you to the ground, asshole, and we'd all pay ten dollars to see him to do it."

I should point out that we print journalists harbored quite a bit of resentment and contempt for television news gatherers for several reasons: they were pushy and arrogant, they could actually change the story by making politicians and others act differently because cameras were rolling (politicians would sometimes elbow five print reporters out of the way to get to a camera, to which they were drawn like moths), and they usually just skimmed the top of the story and let us do the real reporting. Often they'd just read our stories on the air after we had done the work. We were also jealous that on-air reporters tended to be much better coiffed, groomed and dressed than us scraggly notebook-toters, so there was little love lost between us.

The TV ruckus raised the tension in the air closer to the boiling point—and it was very different from the giddy, hopeful kind of tension that precedes a field goal attempt on the last play of the championship game. There was violence in the air, and it was ugly. Nervous, frustrated, angry men on both sides of the law were aiming loaded weapons at human beings, and darkness was descending like a shroud. Night creatures began to scratch and call in the woods.

Only moments after the dust-up with the television crew, deputies apparently told Mrs. Elroy and Taylor's brother that they needed to confer with them in a police van a good seventy-five yards from the hostage car. Sonny snapped a few shots of them through his black, trumpet-sized lens. I saw a deputy watching their progress, and when they were safely out of the way, he told the sheriff. Ledbetter nodded his head—negotiations had failed and he felt he had no choice. He gave the order.

Two men carrying high-powered rifles and dressed more like weekend hunters than police officers emerged from the clump of lawmen. One of the shooters crouched low to the ground and hustled to a spot behind a squad car no more than thirty feet from the car, in a position to look over Taylor's left shoulder. The other walked slowly toward the car from the other side, keeping a huge pine tree between him and Taylor. They had obviously planned the attack meticulously, because they raised their guns almost simultaneously, took aim, and fired within a tenth of second of each other, *bam! bam!*

Taylor jumped, and I saw his arm flail at the roof of the car. I would later learn from relatives that the first shots had missed, and that Taylor's final words to his wife were, "They're shooting at us." The driver's side door flew open and Taylor's wife lunged to the dirt, clawing away on the ground. Her feet had barely cleared the door when a deputy ran to her, shielded her body with his, scooped her to her feet and half-carried, half-dragged her to safety. Meanwhile, about seven more deafening shots blasted the stillness, and a spray of auto glass splashed through the air. During that fusillade, I saw Taylor's feet kick the windshield once and then collapse. He had apparently slunk down in the seat and put his feet on the dash, trying to make as small a target as possible.

When the shooters paused, someone yelled "Go!" and several deputies rushed the car from both sides, aiming their service revolvers into the front seat and yelling "Drop the gun! Drop the gun!" When they came out of their crouches, raised their weapons and clicked the hammers to safety position, we all knew they'd been yelling at a corpse.

There was a moment of stunned silence as the roar of rifle-fire still echoed in our skulls and we all realized we'd just witnessed an execution. A despondent man who had been talking to his wife twenty seconds before was now a crumpled wad of blasted, bloody flesh. The experience was sobering, to say the least; but that empty, reflective moment was the quick calm before a storm of chaos.

While the gun smoke still hung in the air, I heard the pounding steps of a man running and saw Taylor's brother sprinting through the crowd toward the car. Somebody yelled to stop him, and several deputies grabbed him just before he got to the car. They pushed him back, trying to be as gentle as possible with a man who had every reason to be distraught and enraged.

At the same time, Meatball had plowed through the lawmen straight to the car and taken two flash photos of the dead man before Ledbetter barked an order and deputies pounced on him. He struggled, yelling about his rights, as they pushed and pulled his beanbag body away from the car. When they finally let go of him, Meatball found himself in even more inhospitable environs. When he shouted that he had a right to photograph "the dead guy," the dead guy's brother ran about ten feet and pole-axed him with a vicious right and followed it with several more roundhouses to the head and shoulders before deputies could separate them. Violence vibrated in waves through the charged air.

Meanwhile, the television crew was emboldened by the distraction and headed for the death car. When they were about thirty feet from it and closing fast, the cameraman had to turn on the blazing lights, and it lit up the place like a locomotive. Journalistic hell was breaking loose. Ledbetter barked orders, more scuffling ensued, deputies grabbed TV people, and I didn't know how long it would be before it would be open season on all reporters.

"Get their film! Get all the film!" I heard a deputy shout, and armed and uniformed officers quickly fanned out looking for cameras. Oh, crap. I hurried to an unoccupied pickup truck and put my camera in the back under a piece of plywood to buy some time, to see if they were actually going to follow an order that clearly violated the Constitution. About that time, Sonny came walking by, and it was comical to see a 200-pound man with a camera and lens the size of a small mortar trying to look invisible. A deputy blocked his path and said, "Give me your film." Before Sonny could say anything, I whipped out my reporter's notebook to look semi-official and said, "There hasn't been enough light to use that thing for three hours." The deputy was distracted by other reporters with cameras trying to walk away and decided not to waste time with us. He said, "Okay," and took off to stop someone else. Sonny gave me a comical look as if to say, "Lying to the police? You'll get us killed!"

I used my body to screen him from view and told him to take out his film and hide it in his underwear. With a red face, he did it.

I leaned into the pickup truck, quickly removed the film from my camera and the exposed roll from my pocket and hid them in a greasy KFC box at the bottom of a live oak. I grabbed another roll, reloaded and started walking toward the road. I heard a deputy shout "Stop!" behind me, but I honestly didn't think he was talking to me because I had my camera under my t-shirt next to my gut and didn't think anyone could see. He yelled, "I said *stop!*" and I turned to look over my left shoulder just as he was coming around to my right. When I turned back and found him, he had a shotgun leveled at my stomach, and that familiar frozen flower bloomed in my chest. He was mad. "You deaf, boy!? I told you to stop!"

"Yes sir," I said, keeping my hands raised really high. "I'm sorry, sir, I didn't know you were talking to me."

"Is they film in that thang?" he said in fluent redneck, flicking his chin at it.

"Well," I hesitated, obviously stalling.

"Take it out and give it to me, right now," he said in a tone that matched the seriousness of the shotgun still pointed at my gut. Nothing takes me out of an argumentative mood any faster. I removed the blank film and gave it to him, looking thoroughly disappointed. At least he asked my name and what paper I worked for, and I later found out that they actually identified most of the film they confiscated.

Meanwhile, Sonny had made it another thirty feet, and just as I caught up with him another deputy stopped him and demanded the film. In a cracked and nervous voice, I heard Sonny say, "There ain't been enough light for three hours to shoot with this one." The cop demanded the film anyway, and Sonny pretended to rewind it, then popped it out and gave the blank film to him. As we walked toward my car, I gave him my camera and told him to wait for me.

I waded back into the cop swarm without my

camera, wielding my notebook, asking questions. The deputies told me they couldn't comment, which was absolutely true—Ledbetter would have hung them by their boots if they'd said a word. In the swirl of post-shooting chaos, Ledbetter was too busy with police work to be concerned with the press. He had a deputy announce that no more information would be released today, that the sheriff would have a statement at noon tomorrow. A collective groan went up, and I fell in with a couple of other reporters walking back to their cars who were complaining bitterly about the skimpy information they had to write a story. I was moaning along with them when suddenly my trick ankle gave out on me and I sat down, coincidentally, next to a KFC box beside a live oak. I told them to go ahead, that the ankle would quit hurting in a few minutes. As soon as they were gone, I retrieved the film, slipped it into my socks and headed for the car.

My deadline was only an hour away, and it was at least a 45-minute drive to the office. This was in the days before cell phones, and there wasn't a pay phone within ten miles. I dropped Sonny at his car, and he said he'd put the pedal to the metal and try to beat the deadline. He thought he might have time—they could develop and print with astonishing speed—but there was no way I could drive to the office and write the story in time.

As I drove down dark State Road 57, with nothing but woods on either side for miles, I knew my options had narrowed to one. I finally saw the lights of a residence, pulled into the driveway of a neat little country home, quickly got into my shirt and tie and knocked on the door. An older man answered without opening the door, and I explained my situation. I asked him to look at my official Press card that I had pressed against the front window. He studied the card and me for a minute, then said he was sorry but he just couldn't allow somebody he didn't know into his house at night. I told him he could hold his gun on me the whole time if I could just use his phone to call in my story, and he said he didn't like aiming his gun at nobody.

I told him who my parents were, and my uncles and aunts, and a few cousins who lived in the general area, who my grandparents were, and he stopped me: "Mack Cumbest the hospital trustee?"

I said, "Yes, sir, he's my papaw on my mama's side," and I quickly recited my grandparents' phone number and told him he could call them if he'd hurry but that I was running out of time and might lose my job, and he said he figured it would be all right for me to use his phone for a few minutes, that him and Mr. Mack was in Masons together.

After I called in the story to an ecstatic city editor, I drove into the office to see if Sonny had made it in time—and to collect a few kudos from my editor, of course. After Sonny told the editor about the wholesale film confiscation, he actually held the presses for almost fifteen minutes—a rarity since it throws the distribution schedule off—so we could run a couple of pretty good shots Sonny had taken of Taylor holding the gun in the cemetery and a cop with a rifle behind a squad car. They weren't great, but we were pretty sure they'd beat anything the competition had and we were right.

At ten p.m., the editor and I tuned into the Biloxi station, and Sonny went to another TV to see what the crew from Mobile had gotten. When the Biloxi station led their *Eyewitness News* with a hospital expansion story, we let out a whoop—they obviously had little or nothing on the biggest story of the day. When the anchorman finally got to the police shooting, the report was so ludicrously vague—something happened that led to the police shooting somebody, but they didn't know who it was nor why—that my editor guffawed and pounded his desk in amusement. A moment later Sonny came in from the other room with a big grin. The reporter out of Mobile had filled all of ten seconds with the facts he knew about the shooting, and then burned about two minutes reporting the horrifying way he and his crew were mistreated by the police officers. They had practically none of the facts or background of the story. The next morning, anyone who wanted to know the details of the police shooting near the county line—and thousands did—would have to buy a *South Mississippi Sun.*

Again, Ratface gets some of the credit. Had I not endured a terrifying experience in a foreign jail, I'm not sure I'd have had the moxie, resourcefulness, or clear-headedness under fire to do what had to be done to get the story. Of course, I foresaw no such silver lining when I was washing out my underwear in a concrete tank in a prison yard.

Chapter Fifteen:

Goat Butt Soup and Good News

One day when Loudspeaker was honking away, I was watching the Europeans watching the old guard's lips when I heard him trying to make an *M* sound and a *D* sound, and the loudspeaker yelled, *MUKAKA DURODNAN!!* My heart fluttered. I took off my cap, scuttled over and asked if I could see the name. It was mine. He smiled, said, "Chee-cah-go!" and pointed at a spot on the ground. That meant I was to wait there and he'd take me where I needed to go. I stood on my spot, listening to the loudspeaker howl, taking deep breaths, and praying to God that Ratface was somewhere doing the same thing—breathing.

The old man gathered about half a dozen of us scraggly specimens and led us out of the yard and beyond the big wall into a maze of corridors. The prison looked about four million years old. The brick was worn, the hinges and bars encrusted with ancient rust. We turned a corner, I heard people screaming, and that itchy caterpillar of alarm crawled up my spine. Screaming rarely portends anything good, it seems to me, but our chaperone didn't seem to notice. As we got closer, I could hear women's voices. We passed a courtyard and

Not all "experts" are PhD's—or even literate. I listened to anyone who knew something I didn't.

I got to see Moroccan Visitation. There were two chain-link fences about six feet apart and topped by barbed wire. Behind the near fence stood about twenty prisoners. Behind the other stood twenty or twenty-five visitors, most of them women. A guard with a nightstick walked slowly up and down the space between the fences. The prisoners and the visitors—about fifty souls—screamed at each other as loudly as they could, trying to be heard over the ear-splitting caterwauling. If you wanted to have an intimate conversation with your loved one, you were ludicrously out of luck. On the other hand, if you wanted to arrange to smuggle in contraband, you had to scream it past a guard four feet in front of you. Of course, my theory was that the guard was the only deaf one on the staff.

I saw people weeping on both sides of the fence. Having loved ones that close and unable to touch them must be painful, and the frustration of being six feet away from someone and literally not being able to yell loud enough for them to understand you must be maddening. I prayed that their legal system was a little more organized.

*   *   *

It was strangely comforting to be ushered into a small office that looked like any county office in Mississippi—dingy beige walls, a desk cluttered with kids' photos, beige bookshelves, a beige filing cabinet—and a chubby man behind a the desk wearing a white short-sleeved shirt and a blue tie! I was secretly thrilled that he wasn't a hookah-smoking *mullah* with a dagger stuck in his sash. He put on a pair of reading glasses and suddenly bore a striking resemblance to Mr. Moody, my seventh grade math teacher. I wanted to stay in his office and just look at him for awhile.

He looked over the papers in my file, then

looked over his glasses at me. His eyes sparkled with amusement. "Monsieur Dryden," he said in French, "did you come to Morocco to be a tourist or a gangster?"

I grinned weakly and said, "A tourist, I assure you, sir. The man I fought was not a nice man."

My chubby man's Santa Claus demeanor hardened a bit. "You cannot come into our country and beat our citizens just because you don't think they are *nice*, Monsieur Dryden. Do you know how we deal with violent people in our country? It is very different than in America, where people beat each other like cowboys and gangsters every day with no consequences."

"I'm very sorry for what I did," I said, very sorry for what I did. I couldn't *stress* how sorry I was for what I did. I didn't want to come across as one of those jerks who "showed no remorse." This might be my only chance to show it, so I showed *lots* of remorse—I showed him advanced stages of remorse. "I'm truly very, very sorry for what I did, sir, but I felt I had to defend myself. He was—" I didn't know how to say "pushy slimeball" in French, so I settled for "very angry and aggressive."

He smirked. "He says the same about you."

The sharp splinter of ice that had been lodged in my heart suddenly melted. I was overcome. Through tears and with a choking voice I said, "He-he's been talking, really?"

"Of course he has," the man said, surprised at my emotion. "He wants you to be put away forever. You nearly killed him. What did you expect?"

"They told me—in the jail they told me—" I couldn't force the words out over the bubble in my throat, so I just shook my head, tears streaming into my mouth and dropping onto the floor. I knew I could trust this humble government servant. I let the tears flow, the ice garrote that had been choking me for almost two weeks melting away in rivulets.

He mumbled something in Arabic that I didn't understand, but the tone was clear: "Why do those jerks at the jail get their jollies terrifying foreigners? What's the point? Petty little minds, bah!"

In French, he said, "He's quite alive and not feeling charitable towards you, Monsieur Dryden. I can't guarantee what the judges will decide, but you are lucky that this man causes trouble often and is not a stranger to the police. I don't expect you'll be our guest much longer," he said. Then he smiled and the gold in his teeth glittered. "But while you are in our country, you mustn't act like Clint Eastwood or it will not be good for you. Good day."

Faced with another split-second decision, I went with my instinct *not* to kiss him on his adorable little nose. I didn't offer my hand, either, but I did manage to thank him about forty-seven times before he finally waved me *out* already.

I hadn't realized just how heavy the burden on my heart was until it flew off and I nearly floated out of my shoes. I'd been occupied full time with coping, I suppose. Ratface was breathing and cursing me! Glory! I could endure months in this place. Years had seemed daunting, decades crushing; but now the proverbial light at the end of the tunnel was glowing warmly.

Even the Goat Butt Soup tasted better that night. I'm pretty sure I figured out the recipe:

Into one 55-gallon drum of dirty water, place one sliced carrot, one chopped onion, some cartilage from the animal of your choice, a pinch of salt, and a handful of leaves from the nearest shrub. Cook for two weeks, then allow to cool. Set a live goat in this mixture for three minutes, or to taste. Remove goat and serve tepid with three-day-old bread.

After a week of this as my nutrition, I was praying for my freedom and a normal bowel movement.

Several of us "Europeans" had met with the same man that day, so we spent the evening interpreting every syllable he'd uttered. The consensus was that most of us were going to be there no more than a couple of months, and we all agreed that we could endure sixty or seventy days without committing suicide or strangling a cell monitor. The Kenyans were looking at a slightly longer stretch, maybe six months. They had been a little too ambitious. Everyone else had been caught with a couple of two-pound bricks or less. The Kenyans had tried to smuggle out about forty pounds of hashish, which was considered greedy. It would take them a few more semesters to graduate from Kasbah Community College.

Chapter Sixteen:

The Revenge of Teddy Bear

Two days later they called for Mukaka Durodnan again and hustled me to a holding area, where
I was handcuffed and outfitted with leg-irons. Three
Moroccan prisoners and I were then loaded onto
a truck and driven about twenty minutes across
town to a municipal building, where we were herded
into another holding room to wait our turn. After a
couple of hours I was the only one left, and I was
alone for another hour or so. I remember trying to
picture what my hearing would be like: a big empty
room with a scowling bear in a velvet burnous at
a desk, a court clerk at another desk, and a guard
behind me. Spectators would have no interest in
my insignificant little nightmare, so there was no
reason for anyone else to be there. Presently two
guards came in and one removed my shackles. They
led me down a hallway to the door of the courtroom,
told me to *guhalla* my *muk*, and pushed open the
heavy door.

I walked into the room and sucked in my
breath as a cacophony of jabbering and an explosion
of colors hit me like an avalanche. The room was
packed, and everybody talked at once. There were
even people standing outside the building looking

through and leaning into several large open windows. I had been in rooms packed with people for about two weeks, but we were a scraggly, dirty, sullen bunch. The courtroom teemed with passionate people in rainbow-striped *djellabas* and burnouses, and their steady yammering filled the room with electricity. I suppose there were lawyers, clerks, defendants, prosecutors, civilians, relatives—everybody who would normally be in a court of law. The seeming disorder was unnerving—I was hoping for more decorum. My sensory overload was already blowing fuses when I saw the men who would decide how long this chapter of my life would be.

Three judges in shiny, bright green robes sat at the front of the courtroom about six feet apart, the one in the middle on a seat slightly higher than the other two. All three looked up from their papers to stare at me without blinking, then went back to reading. I was impressed with their regal presence. I swallowed, reminding myself to look remorseful, not impressed. A young man in Western clothing and carrying a file approached us and told the guard he'd take me from there. He hardly looked at me when he asked in French if I was Monsieur Dryden. I said yes and asked if he was my lawyer. He frowned, shook his head and said something I didn't understand. In fact, his question about my name was about the *last* thing I understood during my "trial."

We were walking to our front row seat when I looked into the second row and saw the beautiful sight of Ratface glaring at me with a cut lip and a bandage on one eyebrow. Rapturous, I resisted the urge to run over and kiss him on his scabby rodent cheeks.

We sat down, the High Judge banged a gavel, we stood up, the court got quiet and we sat down. The High Judge looked at me and started spouting Arabic, apparently describing the charges against me. He finished with a screech and spoke to the Low Judge on his left, whose gestures and demeanor toward me indicated that he was the prosecutor, or the Bad Cop, who would argue that I should be flogged in the square and hung up to dry in a dungeon for a few years. After a minute or so, he pointed into the crowd, and Ratface stood up and started mewling his pitiful story. I didn't have to speak Arabic to guess what he was saying: He'd just returned from prayers and was minding his own business, shopping for healing unguents for his crippled niece and looking for something to donate to the orphanage when suddenly this insane American thug charged out of an alley, shoved him to the ground, and started whaling him for no reason he could fathom. He'd been scarred emotionally as well as physically, and would have to have everything I owned to make him whole again. And if he could contribute to the safety of the public by helping to lock up this Yankee menace for thirty years, he would be honored.

When he sat down, I looked to my advocate or court buddy and asked with my eyes and a gesture if I could dispute Ratface's story. He waved *be patient* at me and turned away.

Now it was the Good Cop's turn. He wasn't so sure Ratface was telling the whole story. He asked him something, and the question made Ratface squirm, shuffle, hem and haw. The Good Cop interrupted him and asked a question that sounded like it had a barb in it. Ratface's snout got blotchy and he squeaked nervously, as if he were saying, "Okay, maybe I did try to sell him something, but is that a crime?" The Good Cop told him to sit down and then directed a question at the room in general. I heard a deep voice say something, and everyone's focus abruptly shifted to a spot behind me.

I turned in my seat and, glory be to Allah, who was standing in the crowd in his nice, clean burnous but Teddy Bear, the big, barrel-chested fabric shop man who'd seen the entire incident! He glanced at me and I placed my hand over my heart, thanking him the only way I knew how.

Teddy Bear started telling the *real* story—he mimed Ratface tugging on me, me trying to pull away, Ratface getting belligerent—and after a minute or so Ratface suddenly stood up and barked something at him. Teddy Bear barked back, the judge banged his gavel, and for a few wild seconds the *cous-cous* hit the fan. Guards approached from both sides of the room and the shouting match stopped. One look at Ratface's scowl told me his choirboy image had been tarnished with a big nasty brush. The Good Cop looked pleased. Teddy Bear was obviously sick of this guy causing trouble in his neighborhood, and Ratface looked like he wanted to slither out a window and into his hole.

Teddy Bear sat down, and the High Judge told the Bad Cop to give his closing argument. I could tell his heart wasn't in it, but he managed a couple of angry gestures and glares at me—Ratface nodded in agreement so hard his snout flapped—before wrapping up. The Good Cop spoke in even tones for a moment, then—while staring at Ratface—said a phrase like a whiny schoolgirl, and a musical chuckle rippled through the crowd. I almost laughed out of relief myself, but decided to play it safe and keep my remorseful face on until I was on a safer continent. After a few more comments, Good Cop raised his palms, done.

The High Judge pursed his lips and made a little show of thinking about it for a moment, looking at his papers, at Ratface, at me, at Teddy Bear. After a few seconds he snorted a short phrase in Arabic and slammed the gavel. Everybody in the courtroom started yakking again and shuffling papers and walking around. My verdict had been handed down, and I didn't know what the heck it was! My court buddy was stuffing papers into a briefcase. I grabbed his arm and said, "What happened?!"

"Oh," he said, apparently forgetting that I wasn't conversant in the native tongue. "*Trois mois sursis*" (prounounced "*soor-see*").

Trois mois? That means *three months!* I blanched and repeated it. God. I was sick. He saw that I was sick and said, "You're not happy with this?"

I looked at him helplessly. "Three months in prison? No, I'm not happy."

He frowned. "No!" he said. "Trois mois *sursis!*"

Sur si? Sourci? I had never heard the word. "*Sourci?*" I said. "*Qu'est-ce que cé?*" What does that mean?

"You don't serve it," he said. "But you go to jail for three months *immediately* if you get into any trouble at all." Ah! Three months *sursis!—suspended sentence!* "You are free," he continued, "but you must leave Fez by sundown tonight, and be out of the country by Saturday."

That gave me three days. I planned to beat that by two and a half days.

*   *   *

I had to bribe a snake-eyed clerk about $50 to get my passport back, but fortunately I had traveler's checks and very little cash when I'd been arrested, so I got off cheap. I even got back my belt and my pocketknife, which shouldn't have surprised me because there are plenty of good, honest people in Morocco. I just tended to run with a rough crowd because of my economic status and my business.

I went to the inn where I'd stashed my backpack and was pleasantly stunned to find that the owner had kept it. He told me that after a week, his son-in-law wanted to sell it all because the American

I didn't know it at the time, but I instinctively used The Formula to meet my most terrifying challenge.

wasn't coming back. "But no!" he shouted, pointing his finger to Allah and puffing out his chest. Seems his defense of my possessions had been quite heroic. He'd valiantly beat back the plundering hordes who tried to sack his establishment every day and steal the American's treasure, apparently risking serious bodily injury on an hourly basis. I registered what I hoped was the appropriate degree of amazement and gratitude, asked to see my stuff, and was thrilled and astonished to find the pack and its contents—even my little Brownie camera—apparently unmolested. I patted him on the back and told him he was the sturdiest security guard and protector of property in all of Morocco, and he seemed mildly pleased. Then I gave him about ten bucks, and his face expanded into a skin-stretching, gold-toothed grin. His dramatic retelling of his defense of my property had apparently worked at least five bucks better than he'd hoped for.

As anxious as I was to flee Fez, I knew I couldn't leave until I at least tried to thank Teddy Bear. I wouldn't have risked tunneling into the *souq* again had it not seemed a sacred duty, but I felt I had no choice. I hit only a couple of dead ends before I found the site of my youthful indiscretion, and was disappointed to find a teenaged boy manning the fabric shop. After some baby French and charades, the boy's eyes lit up with understanding. He jabbered something to the owner of the adjoining shop, motioned for me to wait and went tearing off through the alley. I knew I could be there for awhile, so I gratefully accepted the next-door shopkeeper's offer of a tall glass of hot, sugary tea stuffed with mint leaves.

About an hour later, right on Moroccan time, the boy proudly led Teddy Bear into the shop. The big guy was obviously surprised and gratified that I had bothered to come back just to thank him, and waved off my praise with great modesty. He reluctantly agreed to take a photo with me, and it only took me ten minutes and four sand drawings to explain to the boy how to frame us and push the button. Teddy Bear was a good, honest, solid man, and made me sorry that I hadn't taken the time to get to know more Moroccans like him. I gave him my pocketknife and he, of course, immediately began protesting that he couldn't possibly take it. I made him and the boy laugh when I covered my ears and told them I had suddenly gone deaf and couldn't hear what he was saying. I thanked him once more, and we shook hands and touched our hearts in the Moroccan way. Then I walked to the station and got on the first train north. I didn't know it at the time, of course, but I was just one panic attack away from writing *finis* to this chapter of my life.

Me and my savior, Teddy Bear.

Chapter Seventeen:

Glory Land

I watched the dusty brown fields of Morocco undulate past outside my train window, pleased to put miles between me and Fez. I got off in Tétouan and took the first bus I could get to Ceuta. We were bumping along, passing men on camels, families walking in the dust as the father rode a jackass, men pulling carts full of junk, when I saw a man who reminded me of Ratface. I grinned, pleased that he was some 200 miles behind me. Then a nasty thought hit me like a rock between the eyes. What if Ratface had figured out a way to extract his pound of flesh? What if the man who'd kept my pack at the inn had kept it for another reason? In retrospect, he seemed a little too eager to convince me of his honesty. With the border gates literally in sight, I quickly dumped the contents of my pack out on the seat beside me and turned it inside out to make sure no one had slipped in anything that would cause me complications. Spain and Morocco were different worlds. The authorities in Spain didn't wink at hashish. They put you in a dungeon for years. I tore my pack apart, looking in every crease and fold, feeling the seams and the leather bottom for tell-tale bumps. I was the last person off the bus, and I felt the bus driver looking at me too long. I could only pray I didn't miss a grainy little ticket to a Spanish inquisition.

The guard who looked at my passport and into my pack must have seen my pale lips, so he took his time pillaging my goods. He told me to empty my pockets and take off my shoes. After a camel's lifetime, he finally stamped my passport and showed me the gate, and I had to will myself not to sprint to the other side.

Although I was pretty much a free bird, I couldn't really enjoy the ferry ride across the Strait of Gibraltar. Someone might race up alongside us in a motorboat yelling in Arabic, demanding the Yank be handed over to them. Silly, I know. But I didn't really take a full breath until I stepped off that little boat onto real Spanish soil and realized I was truly free. I sat down in a sunny spot and watched the seagulls swirl in the salty blue air and just talked to God like an old friend for a few minutes. *I was really, really, stupid, Lord. Thanks for giving me a second chance even though I probably didn't deserve it. I'm a stupid, immature hot-head, and I'm really, really going to work on fixing that, I promise. What can I say? I know You were in there with me. Thank You. Thank You.*

I used to wonder if everything that had happened to me was just fate, or completely in God's hands, or if I really had changed the outcome in any way. I decided that I had. For one thing, I know in my heart of hearts that I didn't try to kill Ratface, because I'm not a killer. If I were, I'd have stomped his windpipe shut or broken his neck. I had been taught ways to kill a man, and I never came close to using them. I only wanted to knock him out—the legal, legitimate goal of every boxer who hears Rotarians and attorneys and Sunday school teachers loudly urging him to do just that. I didn't deserve the fate of a murderer because I actually showed judgment and restraint—which I say rather sheep-ishly, of course. Also, decades later, when I began researching the nuts and bolts of goal-achieving, I realized I had instinctively used the ancient formula (*see Chapter One)* to gain the respect I needed to survive long enough to get out of that place in one piece:

1. I controlled my fears—a full time job when you're locked up in a country where the king trumps the constitution and the ACLU is as ridiculous a notion as paying somebody $10 million a year to throw a baseball.

2. Without a positive mental attitude, I'd have been a lunatic blithering in tongues within a week.

3. Identifying a specific goal in survival situations is not the most difficult step—I had to earn respect to keep breathing

4. While shivering in a cell, I created and re-fined every jump, gouge and slash of my plan, then envisioned it repeatedly until it felt automatic.

5. I took bold, dramatic action by staging a "secret" demonstration for a couple of wide-eyed blabbermouths.

6. To say that I was observant while incarcer-ated is an understatement. My eyes and ears were ratcheted up to Full Sensory Intake mode every minute I was in prison. If you didn't pay attention to every sign, every nuance, you'd get your *muk* slammed into your gut before you could *guhalla.* I listened to every word of advice Abdelatif—a con-victed felon and therefore an expert—had to offer for getting through the day in Club Fez.

7. I used every tiny crumb of information I gathered to adjust my behavior every second of every day, like a boxer adjusts to every feint, jab and body shot. In many ways, my fate was in the hands of others. But because I listened, learned,

and acted accordingly, I got the respect that saved me from being brutalized by the unsocialized dregs who end up in jail.

So before we take this train into the station together, I'll get on my soapbox for just a moment and urge you to stop making excuses for not doing that thing you really want to do. You've got a goal that's nagging at you, don't you? Something you keep putting off, or that you think is too difficult or complicated or time-consuming? Stop making excuses right now. Take control of it. Go back to Chapter One and write down The Formula—handwrite it in fat red felt-tip, or type it up and print it out—just get it down. Don't stash it in a drawer or in a To Do One Day file—pin or tape it up where you can see it every day. If others can see it, all the better—some gentle nagging from a friend or loved one can nudge you toward your goal. Write what you're going to accomplish in big letters right beside it. Write a letter to someone who matters to you and tell them not what you *want* to do but what you're *going* to do. Then you'll have a contract, which is much harder to break than a wish inside a daydream.

Let me remind you that you're a day closer to your last on this planet than when you started reading this thin little book. Be bold. Shake things up. You don't want to drag regrets with you into your feeble years. Act while you've still got the energy and resilience to bounce off a few brick walls and get back in the game *(Falling on your face is still moving forward!)* Time's a-wastin'. Get off the couch and go for it.

That's the shortest sermon I've ever preached. I hope it gooses you into action.

*   *   *

I walked to the mechanic's shop, and my sad-sack van looked like Home. I climbed into the back, took my shoes off and realized how tired I was. I flopped down in that wonderfully fluffy sleeping bag and slept for about three hours. When I woke up, even the van wanted to party—when I finally got it to start, it backfired like a celebratory rifle shot.

In downtown Algeciras I found a cozy little eatery with plastic flowers and the Catch of the Day drawn on a blackboard by someone with more enthusiasm than talent. A Grandma and Grandpa couple smiled warmly when I was shown to a table beside theirs. "*Buenas tardes señor, señora,*" I said, and they returned my greeting, probably amused by my fumbling Spanish. *Paella*—a spicy rice and seafood dish I love—was on the menu, so I ordered it and a bottle of semi-expensive Spanish wine. When I poured a glass and started to sip it, I caught myself and stopped—I realized I was violating a universal rule.

I asked the waiter to bring me two more wine glasses, and I sat there mentally constructing a Spanish sentence from my sparse vocabulary. The idea I was going to try to get across was—for me—pretty complex, so it took awhile. When I felt confident, I took the glasses and the wine to the table of the elderly couple, took a deep breath, smiled, and tried my best to say, "Excuse me, but I am celebrating and would be honored if you would drink a toast with me." They looked at me like I had said, "Hi, I'm a gerbil from the planet Plimbo."

Patiently and sympathetically, the man began asking questions, trying to decipher what I was trying to say. I was stumbling through another attempt when an amused younger man at a nearby table said, "*Señor, momento,*" then yelled, "*Roberto!*"

A man in a kitchen apron appeared. The young man explained, Roberto smiled at me and, in English, said, "What are you wishing to say?"

I told him and he translated. The elderly couple smiled broadly and said, "Of course we will drink with you!" and took the glasses.

I asked the younger man and Roberto to join us, and Roberto cheerfully found two more glasses. After filling the glasses, I raised mine and the elderly couple stood for the toast. Then Roberto said, "What are we celebrating?"

I started to say the word, and the bubble swelled in my throat. I smiled even as the first tears dribbled out. I was helpless. My new friends were surprised, of course, but recognized tears of joy and smiled. I raised my glass and said, *"Libertad!"*

They raised their glasses, and with a love of freedom and humanity that no border or language barrier can restrain, shouted, *"Libertad!"*

Epilogue

About six months after my release, my travels took me to Lyon in the south of France. I was driving my van when I happened to glance over at a group of people waiting for a bus. I saw a familiar face, pulled over, and gave Christophe the shock of his life. I hadn't been looking for him. I hadn't even remembered that he lived in Lyon, a city of about half a million. He wasn't the pale, terrified kid I shared bread with in prison. He was an exuberant chatterbox with some color in his face, and he insisted that I come home and stay with him and his family as long as I wanted. I stayed for two days, watching televised *futbol* with his round little Dad, gorging on wonderfully rich dishes swimming in scrumptious French sauces. That second night, his sweet little bird-like Mom prepared a spectacular lamb curry feast, and I waddled off to take a hot bath. Luxuriating in the hot water, enveloped in a cloud of lilac-scented bubblebath, I couldn't help thinking that I was living proof that what goes around comes around.

Epilogue to the Epilogue

I asked a few of my friends to read the book before it went to press and give me notes. Surprisingly to me, several of them asked if the epilogue about Christophe was "really" true. I suppose they thought I might throw in a tall tale to end the book warm and fuzzily. I didn't. I wouldn't retell it if it weren't true, because it's the only thing interesting about it.